THE VISION O
THE CHILD

By
Fr. Emile A. Ladouceur, M.S.

image omitted

La Salette Communications Center Publications
947 Park Street
Attleboro, Massachusetts 02703
Website: www.lasalette.org

Imprimi Potest:

Very Rev. Fr. René J. Butler, M.S., Provincial Superior
Missionaries of Our Lady of La Salette,
Province of Mary, Mother of the Americas
915 Maple Avenue
Hartford, CT 06016-2330, USA

Nihil Obstat:

Humberto S. Medeiros, S.T.D.,Chancellor

Imprimatur:

James L. Connolly, D.D. Bishop of Fall River Fall River, Massachusetts April 14, 1956

The nihil obstat and imprimatur are official declarations that a book or pamphlet is free of doctrinal or moral error. No implication is contained therein that those who have granted the nihil obstat and the imprimatur agree with the contents, opinions or statements expressed.

Printed in the United States of America

Credits:

Cover and Book Design: Jack Battersby and Fr. Ron Gagne, M.S.
Editor: Fr. Ron Gagne, M.S.
Cover Visuals: from La Salette Rome Archives.
Text Illustrations: La Salette Communications Center Publications, Attleboro, MA, USA.

First Edition: Original manuscript copyright © 1956, by Fr. Emile Armand Ladouceur, M.S. Manufactured in the United States of America, Library of Congress Catalog Card Number: 56-10542

Second Edition: Copyright © Sept. 19, 2016, by Missionaries of Our Lady of La Salette, Province of Mary, Mother of the Americas, 915 Maple Avenue, Hartford, CT 06106-2330, USA

ISBN: 978-0-9828480-7-4

Note from the Editor, Fr. Ron Gagné, M.S.: As editor of this revised edition of Fr. Ladouceur's book, *The Vision of La Salette,* I have gratefully used many historic and more recent La Salette visuals, graciously shared from our own La Salette Archives in Rome, Italy, as well as from the Archives of the Diocese of Grenoble, France and several other sources. We hope that these visuals may help readers to immerse themselves more easily into the life and times of this blessed event.

To My Sisters Helen, Lillian and Leona

Foreward

Well over a century ago, the world echoed with a startling report from the lips of two Alpine shepherds of Dauphiny, France. These plain, unschooled children, Melanie Mathieu and Maximin Giraud, were the witnesses of the Appearance of Our Lady on the Mountain of La Salette, September 19, 1846. The story of the Vision they saw and the recital of the message they heard from the Beautiful Lady spread like wildfire and caught the fancy of a cold, skeptical age.

Thousands upon thousands of people from all walks of life and all parts of the world flocked to the site of the famed Apparition and listened to the story these unassuming children related. Every word they spoke was jotted down and every detail of their recital was critically examined. Civil authorities intervened, and a judicial inquiry was set up by Monsignor Philibert de Bruillard, Bishop of Grenoble, in whose diocese the event took place.

As a result of this inquiry Bishop de Bruillard issued a Doctrinal Mandate (September 19, 1851) declaring the truth of the Apparition "indubitable and certain." The following year, on May 1, 1852, he announced his project for the erection of a Sanctuary on the site of the Apparition. This Shrine he entrusted to the Missionaries of Our Lady of La Salette, a group of diocesan clergy who

— 4 —

later became a Pontifical Religious Congregation with world-wide expansion.

The press in France and abroad reported the fact and the ensuing controversy. Official reports were printed and translated and innumerable documents and testimonies were authenticated, so that perhaps no other event of the nineteenth century has been so minutely recorded for posterity. As a result, there is on hand a wealth of historical data whereby we may reconstruct the children's report with the utmost precision and clarity.

In the archives of the Mother House of the Missionaries of Our Lady of La Salette, in Rome, is a rare volume compiled by Abbé Antoine Bossan, M.S. (1825-1890), one of the first members of the La Salette Missionaries.

It is a time-seared manuscript, carefully bound, containing the early history of the Apparition. Its yellowed pages, now almost transparent, are covered with very neat, fine handwriting. Though written in 1863, the voluminous script still retains its quaint charm and pristine freshness, and since that date little has been published concerning the event of La Salette that has added anything substantially new to this original record. From this treasured document we are enabled to visualize, step by step, the dramatic scene witnessed by the little shepherds of La Salette. One might even draw from Abbé Bossan's work the basic material for a motion-picture scenario.

Abbé Bossan was not immediately involved in the events that followed the Apparition of La Salette. He was not among those who heard the first recitals from the children themselves. However, he made a thorough and tireless investigation of all the evidence that accumulated after the event. Monsignor Joseph Rousselot (1785-1865), Vicar General of Grenoble, gave him free access to his private library. At his disposal were a fine collection of books and pamphlets and the pertinent documents of the diocesan archives. Pen in hand, he copied and checked the various relations, manuscript and printed, which were available at the time.

Among the contemporaries whose testimonies he obtained by word of mouth or by writing were Abbé Mélin, the Curé of Corps, Abbé Jacques Perrin, the Curé of La Salette, Baptiste Pra and Pierre Selme, the shepherds' masters, Mr. Peytard, the Mayor of La Salette, Sister St. Thecla, the children's teacher, and a host of others. Several times after 1860 he met and questioned Maximin. In all his interviews he showed an extreme concern for exactness and authenticity. By collating his various sources it can be ascertained that he never altered the documents that he transcribed.

Abbé Bossan gave proof of solid judgment when he sorted and appraised the many relations that came under his scrutiny. He concluded that the narratives that were written at the children's dictation were exact and complete; those written from memory or in haste were often abridged and less reliable. Likewise he observed that many of the earliest reporters were more interested in the detailed portrayal of the Beautiful Lady than in the accurate transcription of her discourse. Yet most of the relations contained the main facts of the Apparition and only a few reflected a willful distortion of the children's words.

He also noted that whenever the children were asked to tell the story of the Apparition they were content merely to repeat the words of the Lady's discourse, with no more ado or comment. Only when they were plied with questions did they amplify their report. The girl Melanie was more closely questioned than Maximin, for the simple reason that she was the older of the two, and more attentive and more observant, whereas the boy, true to form, was restless and got easily bored during long and wearying sessions.

By dint of prolonged and patient research, Abbé Bossan collected twenty-eight of the original relations of the Apparition, fifteen of which were in manuscript form. The few that he could not unearth or utilize were of little importance. Among the outstanding reports consulted and inserted in his work are the following:

> 1. The handwritten report of Baptiste Pra, the employer of Melanie, the girl witness of the Appari-

tion. This record is dated September 20, 1846. It contains Melanie's account, which she dictated on the Sunday following the day of the Apparition. It was the first relation ever set down on paper in the presence of witnesses, and it is the most exact report of Our Lady's discourse to the children.

2. Abbé François Lagier's report, dated February, 1847. Abbé Lagier (1806-1859), a native of Corps, took down the most complete and the most exact account of all. He had a perfect understanding of the local dialect. His work was done under the best conditions for careful inquiry. He wrote his report at leisure and at a time of year when the children were no longer assailed by the thousands of demands of pilgrims. The witnesses were therefore more at liberty to answer exactly all the questions and objections presented to them.

Abbé Lagier wrote everything under their dictation. He was all the more strict and impartial in his painstaking task, as he himself was then incredulous and strongly prejudiced. He interrogated the children very severely and strove to ensnare them in contradictions. Eventually he was obliged to surrender to the evidence, and he became thereafter an ardent champion of Our Lady's Apparition. His autograph notes fill a considerable volume. Authentic copies of the original are available for historical research. The English translation of Abbé Lagier's report was published under the title, *The Abbé Jots It Down*, La Salette Press: Altamont, N.Y., 1946.

3. Abbé Lambert's account, dated May 29, 1847, contains the recitals of Melanie and Maximin in the patois, or local dialect, of both. The report is as valuable as that of Abbé Lagier and has been

incorporated in the conclusive work of Monsignor Rousselot, which obtained the official approbation of Monsignor Philibert de Bruillard, Bishop of Grenoble.

From a vast storehouse of rich material, Abbé Bossan built an imposing monument of rare historical value. He arranged the various narratives into a skillfully designed mosaic, giving us a composite picture of the event that took place at La Salette. His synthesized report is a coordinated fusion of the best relations extant. Line after line, the words of the witnesses are set into a synoptic tableau. Melanie's and Maximin's recitals are presented side by side, the more easily to be confronted.

In publishing the English translation of Abbé Bossan's *History of the Apparition*, we have adhered to his procedure, which seldom varies: first, we have given the textual script of the children's narrative, then the commentary on each section.

There is no denying the power of the authentic text to establish the truth of the marvelous event of La Salette. Even so, the translator has deemed it helpful to supplement Abbé Bossan's history with a special study of the children's role during the Apparition. This new appraisal casts a strong light on their testimony. The analysis of their character and of their alert and trustworthy reactions as witnesses forms a fitting sequel, under the title, "As They Saw Her."

Many people entertain the notion that there were three distinct appearances of Our Lady at La Salette. This impression may be due to the manner of representing the three various phases of the same Vision. Moreover, since the witnesses of La Salette were shepherd children, as were also the witnesses of Lourdes and Fatima, the event of La Salette is sometimes confused with those two appearances. The story of La Salette as reported in this book will dispel this confusion. It will reveal that the Vision of La Salette was the first of three major Marian manifestations which marked the span of a century, and that the Message it brought to people was developed and emphasized in the later Visions of Lourdes and Fatima.

May this volume, dedicated to Our Lady Reconciler, make known afar her Merciful Apparition, which rightly has been called the Grace of a Century.

Fr. Emile A. Ladouceur, M.S.

February 11, 1956

The two children napped near the bed of the ravine

TABLE OF CONTENTS

Part One – Prelude to Rapture

Heralds of the Queen: Melanie and Maximin

Melanie Mathieu was born at Corps (Isère), November 7, 1831. At the time of the Apparition she was not quite fifteen years of age. For five years previous to the event, she had served as a hired hand. She was engaged as a cowherd, six months before the Apparition, by Baptiste Pra, landowner in the hamlet of Ablandins.

The girl had received little instruction of any kind and she even had scant knowledge of the French language. She possessed the most ungrateful memory; she could retain hardly a word of her catechism. She seldom went to church, being obliged to tend her cattle on Sundays as on any other day.

The girl Melanie was small, puny, and weak for her age. She was extremely timid, remiss, and moody, but she was also meek, modest, and candid. Despite her ignorance of religion, she was exempt of any grave and noticeable defect. Her sweetness of temper and her modest reserve marked her as a particularly innocent child.

Maximin Giraud was born at Corps, August 27, 1835. He was eleven years old at the time of the Apparition. He lost his mother at an early age. He lived with his father, a blacksmith, at Corps. He had not attended school and could neither read nor write. He first began to serve as a hired hand on September 14, 1846, when Pierre Selme, a landowner of Ablandins, engaged him to replace a sick shepherd.

Maximin was a giddy sort of lad, lightheaded, lively, generous to a fault, and very fond of play. He was quite remiss in religious duties, his love of amusement leading him to neglect prayer and Sunday Mass. He was small of stature, slim, and fairly handsome. Unlike Melanie, he was sprightly, bold, frank, without constraint, and altogether free and easygoing. There was no malice in his candid soul.

Such were the channels, so to speak, the instruments that the Blessed Virgin used to transmit to her people the various teachings she brought to earth in her Apparition.

She could hardly have chosen children who seemed less capable and more naturally unfit for the great mission she confided to them. "God chose the foolish of the world to shame the wise, and God chose the weak of the world to shame the strong..." (1 Cor. 1:27). He chose weakness and nothingness to achieve his greatest wonders. This he has shown in the choice of his Apostles, the pillars of his Church, teachers of the world.

Such then were the witnesses, Melanie and Maximin, whom the Blessed Virgin chose to be the heralds of her Apparition. At their voice, hundreds of thousands of pilgrims hastened from all parts of the world to climb the Holy Mountain, until then unknown even to the surrounding regions; at their voice, a splendid Basilica was raised on a height where before only a shepherd's hut could be found. Considering the wonders performed throughout the world by the instrumentality of these two children, we are forced to exclaim, "The finger of God is there!"

> *For the life story of Melanie and Maximin see The Story of La Salette by the Rev. James P. O'Reilly, M.S.; Light on the Mountain by the Rev. John S. Kennedy; and The Children of La Salette, by Mary Fabyan Windeatt.*

THE HOLY MOUNTAIN

The mountain of the Apparition is situated in the Commune of La Salette, about three miles from the parish church. The territory of this Commune forms an immense gap, in the heart of which is set the village church. The population of the village numbered seven hundred souls. The mountain, which rises to a height of 5,400 feet above sea level, is encircled by a range of other mountains, much higher still. The place where the Blessed Virgin appeared was called Dessous-les-Baisses (Below the Slope) because of the declining ridge that joins Mount Gargas and Mount Chamoux. Mount Planeau extends at a right angle from this slope.

The mountain of the Apparition was a wild, isolated spot known only to the shepherds of the region, a hundred years ago. It rises above the timber line and is covered with turf and mountain flowers during the fair-weather season. At the lower slope of Mount Gargas, near the rising ridge of Mount Planeau, a small mountain brook called the Sezia flows into a narrow ravine.

Narration: Meal at the Mountain Spring

Melanie: *That Saturday, when the noon hour struck, we took our cows to drink in the ravine of Dessous-les-Baisses. We sat on the mound while they slaked their thirst at the brook. We then drove them across the brook and made them climb an elevation on the slopes of Mount Planeau. We went to the "Men's Spring" where we sat down on stones which lay on either side. We took our lunch near the spring, talking and eating at leisure.*

Maximin: *At noon we took our cows to drink. Then they climbed up a slight elevation. We took our lunch quite close to the spring, on stone benches which the shepherds had set up.*

Only after the noon Angelus had sounded from the village church of La Salette did the two cowherds leave their masters' fields, which lay about 300 yards from the site of the Apparition. They reached the ravine of the Sezia at ten or fifteen minutes past twelve. This was not the first time the children had met previous to the Apparition. On Monday, September 14, the boy Maximin went to Pierre Selme's house, in the hamlet of the Ablandins in the Commune of La Salette, to replace a sick cowherd for the week. The girl Melanie had been employed six months already in the service of Baptiste Pra, another landowner of the same hamlet. Between Monday and Thursday of that week Maximin had met Melanie only casually, if at all, at the Ablandins, since on those four days the two cowherds tended their cattle in different pastures, far apart. Thursday evening they met and spoke for the first time at the Ablandins. This was their first real acquaintance.

On the next day, Friday, September 18, they watched their cattle together in nearby pastures on the slopes of Mount Planeau. That evening they drove their cattle home together to the Ablandins and on taking leave they made this friendly challenge to each other: "Tomorrow we'll go up the mountain again – we'll see who gets up first."

That Saturday morning Maximin was up early and, mindful of the challenge, he went to fetch Melanie at her master's house. They started off after breakfast accompanied by Maximin's master, Pierre Selme, who was to mow his hay-patch on the side of Mount Planeau. Each of the children led four cows. Maximin took along a mountain goat which belonged to his father. With him also was the mongrel pup, Lou-lou. This dog often shared the generous lad's meager provisions. The day was fair and magnificent, the sky spotlessly clear – a rare occurrence in these mountains at this time of year.

During the forenoon of September 19, 1846, Maximin and Melanie each tended their cattle in their respective masters' fields. These pastures lay about a hundred yards apart on the southern slopes of Mount Planeau, Pierre Selme's toward the east and Baptiste Pra's more to the west. The cattle were grazing on the stretch approximately level with the circular path which now surrounds Mount Planeau. The children were well within sight of each other and they also could amuse themselves at shepherds' games when their watch permitted such relaxation. All the while, Pierre Selme was swinging his scythe on the grassy slopes some distance below and keeping an eye on the two cowherds.

When the noon hour struck, Maximin's master signaled to the boy to take the cows to drink at the brook of the Sezia. Maximin immediately called Melanie and they drove their cattle toward the Collet. That part of the mountain was called Little Neck because of its very narrow shape. The cows were driven down the ravine and made to drink in a shallow pool which the shepherds of the region had made into a sort of reservoir by means of a small dam made of stones and loose turf. The brook often ran quite dry in the summer, hence this expedient to catch every drop of water available for their cattle. This pool was known as Fontaines-des-Bêtes, or the Beasts' Spring.

While the cattle slaked their thirst, the two children sat looking on from the top of the Collet or Little Ridge. This elevation occupied the space which now lies between the right portal of the Basilica and the Chapel of the Assumption. Already in 1863 the locality had completely changed in aspect due to construction work at the Shrine.

When the cows had finished drinking, the children drove them across the brook to the slope of Mount Gargas. This they did by throwing pebbles or sods in their direction, as was customary, or by shouting at them from their position on the knoll. When the cattle had settled on the sunny slope opposite, the children climbed about thirty yards along the ravine, bypassing the dry bed of the little spring which later became known as the Miraculous Spring, and they reached another spring some ten yards higher. This being the only spring of considerable flow on the mountain, the shepherds and mowers of those parts who resorted to it called it the Fontaine-des-Hommes or the Men's Spring. This spring flowed a few yards away from the brook Sezia proper.

At the Men's Spring, Melanie and Maximin rested on stone benches and partook of their frugal meal. This consisted of a few chunks of dry bread and a bit of cheese. They drank from the mountain spring and chatted softly as they ate. During the meal, three other young cowherds who kept their flocks some distance below also came to drink at the Men's Spring. They were two little boys from the hamlets of Brutineaux and Chabannerie and a little girl from the town of Corps. They chatted a while with Maximin and Melanie and then they returned to their fields. They stayed quite a distance away all the rest of the day, either on the flanks of the Chamoux or along the Gargas.

The children once said that there were no other children that day on the mountain but they spoke of Mount Sous-les-Baisses or Mount Planeau. The weather being so favorable, there were also other men besides Pierre Selme, Maximin's master, mowing hay with a scythe, on neighboring mountains, but out of sight of Mount Planeau.

SIESTA

Melanie: *After eating lunch, we crossed the brook and set our knapsacks upon stones. Having laid them down, we sat on the turf a few steps lower and we fell asleep a little distance from each other.*

Maximin: *After we had eaten we both fell asleep alongside the brook, right near the little dry spring.*

In their recital, the children very often used the word lunch *(gouter)*, meaning dinner. At Corps and in other localities of the region, the meal taken at seven or eight o'clock in the morning is called dinner; the noon meal is called lunch; the afternoon lunch is called "re-lunch" *(regouter)* and the evening meal is called supper.

Dinner over, Melanie and Maximin crossed the brook of the Sezia below the Men's Spring and made for the margin of the little dry spring near which two stone benches were set parallel to each other, about a yard apart. Intending to linger around the spring for a while, they dropped their knapsacks on these stone benches.

Maximin's shepherd's blouse, which he used for a knapsack that day, was laid on the bench above the dry spring, and Melanie's knapsack was laid on the lower bench.

It may be noted that when the Blessed Virgin appeared she was seated on the pile of stones where lay Maximin's blouse. She might have touched it close. As a matter of fact, on the evening of September 19, Maximin told his master, Pierre Selme: "We met a lady. I was afraid at first, I did not dare go and fetch my bread which was near her." The bread here spoken of was the remnant of his dinner, which he had wrapped up in his blouse for want of a knapsack.

The knapsacks worn by the shepherds of La Salette were usually made of thick hempen cloth. Some were made of leather. They were very small. The shepherd boys and girls carried them slung over their shoulders, soldier fashion. They habitually kept them all day, even while playing games. Knapsack and shepherd stick were two inseparable articles with these shepherds.

Having dropped these small bundles on the stone benches, the children sat down on the turf, two or three steps below. They chatted a bit and then insensibly fell asleep in their respective positions. Melanie lay a few yards from the dry spring and Maximin three or four yards further down, almost on the exact spot where now (1863) stands the cross of the Conversation. Maximin's dog lay crouched a few steps below. It seems that the mongrel did not budge hence from the time the children fell asleep until after the Apparition was over. The bed of the ravine where the children slept measured about five yards in width, including the bed of the brook.

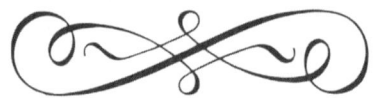

Melanie: *Then I awoke first and I could not see my cows. I immediately roused Maximin and said to him, "Come quick, Maximin,*

let's look for our cows; I cannot see them; I don't know where they are."

Maximin: *Melanie was first to wake up. She then called me and told me to come right over—that we had lost our cows and that we did not know where they were.*

The children remained asleep perhaps an hour and a half. They were never able to compute exactly how long they did sleep. Never before had they fallen asleep while keeping their herds on these mountains. Although it is quite impossible to ascertain at what hour they fell asleep and at what hour they awoke, the children themselves surmised that they went to sleep at about one o'clock and awoke between two and three o'clock.

Melanie was the first to awake. She rose up instantly and threw a hurried glance in the direction of the slope where the cows had rested before she fell asleep. She looked all about the ravine and could not see them. She hastened to rouse Maximin, who slept ever so soundly, and she summoned him to climb the knoll after her. The little boy awoke with a start and, hardly knowing where he was, set out in the footsteps of his companion.

Melanie: *We got up without taking our knapsacks. We crossed the brook and climbed the hillock together, almost in a straight line, in order to find our cows. Having reached the ridge-top, we discovered them all lying down on a small turf-covered plateau, right before us, on the slope of Gargas – they were not far distant.*

Maximin: *And we went looking after our cows. And on turning round we found them lying down on the opposite slope, upon an elevation.*

In their haste and preoccupation, the two children left their knapsacks on the stone benches and simply grabbed their shepherd sticks, which were near at hand. Sometimes the shepherds of these mountains part with their knapsacks to obtain more freedom at games, but they always hold on to their herd sticks. Melanie and Maximin had dropped their knapsacks near the dry spring, but they kept their shepherd sticks ready at hand.

Maximin near his home in Corps

The brook which they crossed was the Sezia. This brook takes its source some 300 yards above the place of the Apparition. It is chiefly supplied by tiny oozing springs along the ravine through which it runs. During summer droughts it readily drains some distance above the miraculous spring. During heavy rains or a great thaw it swells considerably. In normal weather it contains a small volume of water, more like an abundant spring. It is only a few feet wide and has little depth. Its course is north to south and below the site of the Apparition it turns southwest.

The children took a beeline up the knoll and swiftly reached the top, which was some 25 yards above the bed of the brook. They thought that their cattle might be found on the ridge-top, or at least they hoped to discover them from that point of vantage wheresoever they might have strayed. Turning round at this observation point they saw their cattle reclining peacefully on the gentle slope of Mount Gargas, about 60 yards away as the bird flies.

THE BRIGHT LIGHT

Melanie: *Then I said to Maximin, "Quick, let's get our knapsacks and take our cows to pasture." We went down the ravine to fetch* *our knapsacks which we had left a little above the place where we had slept. I went first: Maximin followed two or three steps behind me.*

Maximin: *And we went down for our knapsacks which we had left near the spring.*

As soon as the two cowherds spied their cattle, Melanie was the first to descend from the knoll, just as she had been the first to climb it. Instead of promptly coming down after her, Maximin lingered a while on the summit as if to amuse himself. That is why the little girl said to him: "Come quick now, hurry, and don't be amusing yourself, because it's getting late and we've got to take our cows to pasture right away."

They went down the slope of the ravine where they had slept. They did not descend in a straight line, the way they had gone up, but making a sharp detour, southeast to northwest, they followed the oblique path that led to the Men's Spring, where they had taken their frugal meal. Their knapsacks still lay on the stones near the dry spring, where they had dropped them before falling asleep.

Melanie: *When we were hardly more than halfway down toward the bed of the ravine, I saw a bright light over there, above the stones where our knapsacks lay. It was bright as the sun, much brighter even, but not of the same color.*

Maximin: *And we saw a great light near the spring. Melanie saw it first.*

The children had hardly gone halfway down the knoll, Melanie leading and Maximin a few steps behind her, when the little girl cast a look toward the knapsacks, and on the very spot where these lay she perceived a very brilliant globe of light, of small dimension just then, perhaps three feet in diameter, but later on it was to grow seven or eight times larger.

When Melanie noticed the strange light, she was standing about ten yards from the brook, fifteen yards from the site of the Apparition, and thirteen yards from the spot where they had slept. On their way down from the top of the knoll they had covered about sixteen or nineteen yards. That is why the girl said: "We had scarcely gone halfway down toward the bed of the ravine."

Melanie was first to see the light. This light rested above the stones near the dry spring where their knapsacks lay. It covered both the stones and the knapsacks. It shone like the sun but it was much more vivid, clearer and more dazzling. It was not of the same hue as the sunlight, being so brilliant that the sunlight seemed but a shadow by comparison.

Melanie: *On seeing that, I turned immediately to Maximin and said to him, "Maximin, come quick and see a light over there!" Maximin started to run at once: "Where is it? Where is it?" he said coming near me. "Look over there," I said, my finger pointing toward the little spring. He came by my side and when he saw it he stopped.*

Maximin: *And she said to me: "Maximin, look at the pretty light over there!" I came near Melanie and we both gazed upon it.*

Instantly, Melanie halted, turned on her left toward Maximin, who was following her along the path to the Men's Spring, and told him to come and look at the strange light. In one bound the lad was at his companion's side. Maximin did not at first perceive the light when Melanie called his attention to it. Though he stood practically on the same spot and looked in the same direction as she did, he could see nothing. This explains his repeated query: "Where is it?

Where is it?" It is related that not seeing anything he tapped her on the shoulder and said, "But I see nothing!" Then Melanie pointed her finger toward the little dry spring. At that moment God opened his eyes and he saw the great light.

The other shepherds who happened to be on the heights of these mountains that same day saw no light at the place of the Apparition, though they may have been within the range of vision. Evidently they were quite unaware of what was taking place and God did not allow them to witness it. The two children stood motionless on the spot and considered the luminous globe attentively. However, they were not yet afraid.

Melanie: *At first glance I saw nothing but a very bright light, as if it were a round object scintillating. It seemed to turn and turn incessantly on itself. I could hardly fix my eyes on it, it dazzled them so. To examine it well, we rubbed our eyes every now and then.*

Maximin: *At the beginning we saw nobody in that light.*

At first, Melanie perceived only a brightness, still quite small, extraordinarily brilliant, like a round body scintillating and revolving upon itself with very great rapidity. "When we first saw it it whirled around." The constant movement of the light is described by the children in these peculiar terms of their regional dialect or patois: *bouligava, virava.* "I saw it budge *(bouligava)* a little," said Melanie, meaning that it moved around the same spot. "It shone so brightly that it seemed to rotate *(virava)*." The light in fact did not rotate on itself or anything of the kind, but the brightness produced the effect of a light whirling around. Any luminous body that scintillates strongly will appear to turn with great rapidity before the eyes of the observer who tries to gaze upon it steadily.

Naturally, then, this sparkling globe reacted like a whirling light on the retina of the children's eyes. They imagined that their weak vision hindered them from examining this strange light, and so they kept rubbing their eyes at every instant to clear away a sort of haze which seemed to fill them. Instead of clearing their vision, this seemed to trouble it all the more. At first the light did not sparkle, so that they could fix their gaze upon it, but this lasted only a few seconds. It soon began to scintillate vividly and to blur their vision so that they could observe nothing else until the luminous globe began to part.

The Weeping Mother

Melanie: *Now, after I had told Maximin to come and look, and as I turned around again toward the light to examine it well, I saw it part open as it were almost instantly, and I began to see a pair of hands that grew intensely white. They were raised to a face which they concealed almost entirely. I could not distinguish things very well because the light dazzled me.*

Maximin: *And then it lowered and we saw it part. And all of a sudden we saw a Lady in it.*

After Melanie had called Maximin's attention to the light in the ravine, she turned around again the better to consider it, for she had as yet thrown but a rapid glance at it. Maximin was at her side almost as soon as she had turned around. Instantly, as both looked on, the small, stirring globe of light began to extend in volume until it soon reached the height of an ordinary person. It was now an oblong shape. It seemed to open from within somehow, like curtains that are drawn apart. Melanie said that the light began to extend upward and suddenly parted asunder, revealing a pair of white hands that grew intensely white. In these open hands of immaculate beauty was buried a human face, whose features remained as yet invisible.

On his part, the boy Maximin explained that the light of the whirling globe first lowered, as it were, to the ground at the feet of the Blessed Virgin and then opened apart. The children evidently reported the same phenomenon from a different viewpoint. The light began to extend in all directions and then thinned out at the center of the globe. The witnesses described the light as falling or rising according to the visual angle of their observation. The children always found it rather difficult to make others understand exactly how all this happened. They were never able to make very clear all the details that concerned the person of Our Lady of La Salette.

Melanie: *I had hardly noticed the pair of hands become increasingly white when, instantly, I saw arms and sleeves down to the elbows resting as it were upon the knees. I also saw part of the dress below the elbows – it was brilliant with pearls. I saw before us, upon the stones, as it were, a woman who sat there weeping, her face buried in her hands and her elbows resting upon her knees but I could not see her face nor the rest of her body because the brightness was a hindrance.*

Maximin: *She was seated on one of the stone benches where we had sat. Her elbows were leaning upon her knees and her face was hidden in her hands.*

All the scene of the Apparition unrolled itself before the eyes of the witnesses with instantaneous speed. Scarcely had they seen the light when they immediately perceived the head, hands, and necessarily with great rapidity, arms, sleeves and the rest of the body.

The stone on which the Blessed Virgin sat was a thick slate set over other stones in the form of a bench, on which the shepherds used to take their meal by the intermittent spring. This rough, gray slab was about a foot and a half long, a few inches thick, and proportionately wide. It weighed about 25 pounds. There were two stone benches parallel to each other about a foot and a half from the Miraculous Spring. The Blessed Virgin was seated on the bench placed north, her feet resting in the dry basin itself, a few feet from the head of the spring which ran into the Sezia below.

The Beautiful Lady sat facing south, slightly turned toward the children who were south-southeast of her. When she stood up she faced them directly for a brief moment. She was seated in the attitude of a person overwhelmed by the weight of an immense sorrow. Her body was slightly bent forward, her elbows rested on her knees, and her face was hidden in the open palms of her hands so that her features could not be seen. Under her broad sleeves, which were folded over her forearms, Melanie noticed other narrow sleeves which covered her arms to her wrists. While seated, the Blessed Virgin was already weeping, and when she stood up her face was bathed in tears.

THE CHILDREN'S FRIGHT

Melanie: *We halted when we saw the light. We were afraid. And I cried out at once, "O my God!" And, through fear, I dropped the shepherd stick which I held in my hand. And Maximin said to me: "Keep your stick, now! I hold on to mine and I'll give her a good whack if she does us any harm."*

Maximin: *We saw her both together and as we looked at her, we said not a word to each other. We halted at the same spot when we saw her. We were both afraid. And Melanie went like this: "O my God! What is that?" She dropped her stick and I said to her: "Keep your stick, now! I hold on to mine and if she does us any harm, I'll give her a good whack!"*

The two shepherds saw the Blessed Virgin together, that is, at the same time. Still it seems not impossible that Melanie saw her a brief instant before Maximin, since in this great scene the little girl played the first role in everything. Yet this detail cannot be ascertained because the children always believed that they saw the Blessed Virgin at the same moment. Even if there had been priority of time for Melanie, it could not exceed a few seconds.

The children were still standing at the very spot where Melanie had first noticed the light. When Maximin reached Melanie, they both remained, as it were, rooted to the spot. They were standing about fifteen yards from the Blessed Virgin.

It seems only natural that the two children should have been terror-stricken when they suddenly perceived, in this desert place, so strong and so great a light and within it this extraordinary personage, only partially revealed to them at that moment. They were both frightened – Melanie the more so – but their fright lasted only an instant.

It is not when the children first saw the strange light that fear seized them, but only when they perceived the head and the arms of a mysterious personage within the light. Then Melanie let her shepherd stick fall to the ground. What frightened her was the sight of someone she began to discern.

The children might never have been afraid, or at least less so, if from the very start they had seen the Blessed Virgin entirely and distinctly, for the very rapid development of the globe of light, its extraordinary brightness, and the aspect of a strange person appearing suddenly was all of a nature to frighten not only children but even grown-ups.

Yet the whole tableau of the Apparition unfolded itself so rapidly before them, each scene following in swift succession, that they perceived the Blessed Virgin almost at the same time as the light. Before the Beautiful Lady appeared, Maximin had scarcely taken three or four steps and had thrown only a first glance at the light shown him by Melanie. Everything took place almost simultaneously.

In 1862, Maximin said: "It takes time and plenty of words to describe the scene of the Apparition, but everything unrolled itself so rapidly before our eyes that it all happened as it were in the mere twinkling of an eye. Thus to see the light, first as a small globe, then increasing considerably in size, and to perceive a head, hands, and finally the full person of the Beautiful Lady as she arose, all this took place in perhaps less than a minute."

When Melanie let fall her shepherd stick, the boy Maximin said to her: "Keep your stick!" that is, pick it up and hold it in her hand as he held his, to defend themselves if need be. The shepherd sticks used by the mountaineers of the region are short staves, without iron points, measuring about three feet.

Though Maximin was much younger than Melanie, he was much braver. The girl was naturally very timid and pusillanimous. The boy, on the contrary, was bold and intrepid. The different reactions of the children at the sight of the Apparition were due to natural traits of character, fear and weakness being the endowment of the fair sex.

Telling Melanie to keep her shepherd stick, Maximin assumed a tone of mingled vivacity and menace, in the hope of reproving her for her fear and of rousing her faltering courage. He himself held his shepherd stick uplifted in the attitude of one about to deal a heavy blow. He was on the defensive. This child of eleven was quite determined to strike the unknown personage, whoever it might be, but only in case of attack and of threatened harm to his companion; for it seems that his only thought was to defend her, as may be gathered from the recital reported by Abbé Lagier: "If she does you anything I will give her a good whack." We can portray in imagination the young shepherd David getting ready to attack the giant Goliath, or to defend himself from his attack.

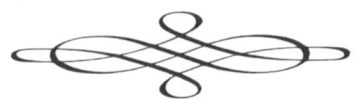

Melanie: *The Lady remained seated until I had shown her to Maximin. He had hardly done speaking when I saw the light rise to a little height and extend somewhat above the head of the Lady as she stood up. She arose almost as soon as Maximin arrived at my side telling me not to be afraid. That is what made me assume that she had been seated.*

Melanie near her home in Corps

Maximin reached Melanie as soon as she had told him to come and see the light, since he was but two or three steps behind her. He noticed the light as soon as she pointed it out to him, and at that very instant the two children perceived the head and the hands of the Blessed Virgin. It was the light and not the Lady that Melanie pointed out to her companion, yet the girl said, "She remained seated until I had shown her to Maximin," meaning that the Apparition revealed itself so swiftly that it seemed to Melanie that she had shown the Virgin to Maximin at the very moment she pointed her finger to the light. When the Beautiful Lady rose from the stone bench, the light around her head gradually extended upward, reaching the height of a person standing. At the same time the light around her person diminished in intensity, and vanished almost entirely at her feet and on the stones whereon she had been seated. This dwindling density of the light enabled the children to perceive the rest of her person down to her feet, and even revealed the dry bed of the spring in which she stood. At first, they had been able to discern only her head and her hands, her arms and her sleeves, and they merely noted her attitude of profound sorrow. When they came close to her they could consider her person more clearly as well as the costume she wore.

Melanie: *Upon rising she withdrew her hands from her face, folded her arms, and immediately came forward in our direction, saying to us, "Come near, my children, be not afraid, I am here to tell you great news." And we were no longer afraid.*

Maximin: *She stood up and advanced a little toward us as we were coming down. Her arms were folded upon her breast and her head was slightly inclined. And she said to us, "Come near, my children, be not afraid, I am here to tell you great news." And we were afraid no more.*

As the Blessed Virgin began to rise, she withdrew her hands from her face. Melanie perceived that her countenance was sad and that her face was bathed in tears. As soon as she stood up she laid her arms one upon the other, right over left, externally; that is, her hands were not thrust one within the sleeve of the other, but each hand was entirely covered by its own sleeve, the border of each sleeve reaching slightly beyond the fingertips. The sleeves were broad and long like those of a nun. She remained thus, her hands entirely hidden and her arms folded, all the while that she spoke to the children and until she disappeared.

Having risen, she came forward at once, a step or two toward the children, intending as it seems to cross the brook before her and to meet them, since they were about fifteen yards away, on the knoll. However, having taken two or three steps in their direction, facing almost directly east, she turned suddenly to her right and descended alongside the brook for the space of about four yards, following a rather southwest course.

She uttered these first words, "Come near, my children," as soon as she began to rise, and she continued to address them with this tender invitation as she advanced toward them. She therefore spoke this whole phrase, "Come near, my children, be not afraid, I am here to tell you great news," first while standing up, then while she advanced toward them and while she turned to her right, and she concluded her invitation only when she began to descend alongside the brook.

When they saw her advance at first in their direction, the two shepherds thought she would go up to them toward the middle of the mound, where they then stood, but as soon as they saw her turn to her right and go along the brook they descended precipitately toward her.

Heretofore, the children could not very well discern who this extraordinary person might be. They could not yet clearly see if it was a woman or not, though the impression grew on them that it really was a woman. Thus far they could only assume that she had been seated in an attitude of profound sorrow. When they saw her arise and walk, they were quite convinced that the person surely was a woman, and when they reached her in the bed of the ravine, they could distinctly consider the Beautiful Lady.

As already mentioned, the two children were on their way down the ravine to gather up their knapsacks when, upon perceiving a great light, they halted in their fright. The Blessed Virgin told them, therefore, to continue their descent and not to be afraid to go down toward the knapsacks, upon which the light rested. She told them she had great news to communicate to them. They thereby concluded that in order to hear her message they must come near her, and they were at her side in a few leaps and bounds.

Until that moment, the children had experienced a great fear, but as soon as they heard the first words of the Blessed Virgin all their fear left them. Not only were they no longer afraid but they were fully reassured and felt, as it were, irresistibly attracted to this Lady. Their hearts were already flooded with unspeakable joy.

THE RENDEZVOUS

Melanie: *As soon as she told us to come near her we promptly came down to the bed of the ravine. We crossed the brook right in front of her and we approached her very close for we could quite have touched her. She advanced to the spot where we had fallen asleep. It was then only that I could clearly see that it was a woman.*

Maximin: *And we came down, crossed the brook and came right near her. We could almost have touched her. She advanced a few steps towards us from the place where she had been seated.*

As soon as the two shepherds heard the words, "Come near, my children," they abandoned the little path to the Men's Spring, in which they stood, and came down almost in a straight line, following the abrupt course they had first taken when climbing up the mound in quest of their cows. They were returning to the spot where they had slept, and toward which, at that moment, the Beautiful Lady was advancing.

The Blessed Virgin descended alongside the brook as far as the very spot where the boy Maximin had slept, where now (1863) stands the Cross of the Conversation. In her descent she followed a northeast-southwest course, and the children were descending directly from east to west. In their progress, the Blessed Virgin and the shepherds traced a sort of acute angle, whose sides, however, were of unequal length.

To reach the Blessed Virgin, the children covered about thirteen or fourteen yards in a straight line. On her part, she walked about four yards, but not in their direction. This shows that she was moving slowly and that the shepherds were coming down in great haste. They crossed the Sezia anew, almost at the very spot where they had crossed it when going up to look for their cows.

Melanie led the way down and she got there first, probably because she was taller than Maximin and ran faster. Naturally she placed herself at the right of the Beautiful Lady. Maximin got there after Melanie and stayed on the side, at Melanie's right, on the brink of the brook and at the left of the Blessed Virgin. They were right near the Queen of Heaven, since no other person could have passed between her and them. During all the time of the conversation they were no more than a foot and a half away from her. From where they stood they could have touched her by simply holding out their hands.

It is only at this moment that the children discerned the womanly form of a Beautiful Lady. Earlier they had assumed the person was a woman, but they were not perfectly sure of it because the exceeding brightness which surrounded her prevented them from distinguishing clearly.

The Blessed Virgin stood in the center of a globe of very strong light, compared to which the sun appeared to them like a mere shadow or seemed at least to have lost its splendor. This globe contained two circles or zones of light. The first zone, the exterior one, was six or eight yards in diameter. In this zone the children stood. The light of it must have reached at least two yards beyond them. This light did not scintillate and was less intense than that of the inner circle. The light of this inner zone, which glowed intensely and sparkled continuously, surrounded only the person of the Blessed Virgin, extending about a foot and a half around her body. This light reached as far as the little shepherds but did not touch them. It is this light that dazzled them and hindered them from seeing clearly.

From the face and the whole body of the Beautiful Lady beamed rays of extreme brightness. These rays weakened insensibly as they reached the circumference of the globe. Had this glowing sphere consisted of natural light, the children might have been scorched on the spot. Nevertheless they remained in its luminous hearth without experiencing the least discomfort. This evokes the biblical incident of the three Hebrew youths in the burning furnace, which became for them a place of cooling delight while the flames might have consumed them (Daniel 3:1-13).

Melanie: *When we both got near her she turned towards us and she placed herself right in front of us. She gazed upon us a very brief moment. While she spoke to us she stood facing the hollow of the ravine and we were facing the summit of the mountain. We placed ourselves right in front of her. We were standing as she was.*

Melanie was the first to reach the Beautiful Lady; Maximin came right after. The two children arrived at the left side of the Blessed Virgin, who at that very moment had her left shoulder slightly turned away from them, since her face was turned almost southwest while the children were coming from the eastern direction. This explains how Melanie, arriving first, placed herself at the Lady's right, leaving Maximin, who followed, to stand at her left.

A better explanation would be that the Blessed Virgin willed it so. As soon as the children came near her she turned slightly to her left, directly south, and naturally stood facing them. The children said, "She placed herself in front of us." If she had not turned toward them a little, the children would have been obliged to advance still farther in order to stand before her. Thus it required a slight movement on the part of the children as well as the Blessed Virgin in order that they might face each other. "She gazed upon us a very brief moment."

As soon as she had turned toward them, the Beautiful Lady first cast a look of tender recognition on the two children, as if to get acquainted with them and inspire confidence. She did not look at them fixedly. After this rapid glance, she lowered her eyes, and kept them lowered all the while she spoke to them.

During her discourse to the children, the Blessed Virgin stood facing southward down the hollow of the ravine in the direction of the flowing brook. The children were facing the summit of the mountain; that is, toward the Col (or Neck) of Mount Sous-les-Baisses at the eastern rise of Mount Gargas, northward. They stood directly in front of the Blessed Virgin, almost touching elbows. The three formed a triangle. The children were not standing at either side of the Beautiful Lady, but in a straight line before her, Melanie to the west and Maximin to the east. They were very close to this good mother. Their low stature obliged the Blessed Virgin to incline her head and shoulders slightly in order to keep the children under her gaze. She did not look at them fixedly in the eye nor even in the face – her gaze seemed only to hover above them.

When speaking to the children, the Beautiful Lady remained standing, with dignity, grandeur and majesty, yet full of kindness, sweetness and affability, so that she inspired the most profound respect and the most tender affection.

While observing this extraordinary majesty and distinction in the person of the Blessed Virgin, the children experienced not the least shyness, embarrassment or timidity. While she bore the marks of celestial grandeur and dignity, there was nothing haughty, pretentious or strained about her. Her very attitude, her bearing, her dress, her tone of voice were remarkably plain, attractive and becoming.

The children held their shepherd sticks in their hands all through the discourse of the Blessed Virgin. Melanie stood, quite modest and respectful. The giddy and lightheaded Maximin, as always, behaved rather distractedly. He did not at first remove his hat until a certain reverential urge impelled him to take it off. He did casually replace it on his head, but most of the time he stood with head uncovered. Unable to stay motionless for any length of time, he amused himself now and then by twirling his hat on his shepherd stick or by knocking pebbles with his stick in the dry bed of the brook. He was just acting true to form, a none-too-courteous country lad.

The Blessed Virgin bore it all until the very end without uttering a single word of complaint and without betraying the least displeasure. When later on someone chided the boy for his lack of politeness, his only defense what that he had not known who the lady was and that, had he known, he would have been on his best behavior. The wonder of it all is that in spite of amusing himself and appearing so distracted during the Blessed Virgin's discourse, the lad retained every word spoken by the Divine Mother just as faithfully as did Melanie, who listened most attentively.

During her discourse to the children, the Blessed Virgin appeared profoundly sad. She wept. Each of the children was witness to her tears. She spoke first in French, then in patois, or the local dialect, and she ended her discourse in French. The French she spoke was plain but correct and elegant. While she spoke she held her arms folded over her breast, and she made no gesture with her hands and no movement of the head.

During all this mysterious colloquy, Maximin's dog remained lying a step or two behind him. At no time during the whole Apparition did he budge or bark – even when the children moved about and while the Blessed Virgin spoke to them he seemed totally unaware of any sound or movement. This otherwise keen and watchful dog was, as it were, riveted to the spot, though the light of the Apparition reached and even enveloped him and though the Blessed Virgin spoke audibly for nearly half an hour. Some have pointed out that this immobility of the shepherd dog made him a silent yet eloquent witness of the supernatural occurrence. To many people this dumb testimony is worth more than other proofs of the authenticity of the Apparition.

MARY'S TEARS

Melanie: *She wept all the while that she spoke to us. I did see the tears flow from her eyes—they flowed in a steady stream.*

When the children first perceived the Blessed Virgin, she appeared to them like a woman overwhelmed by the weight of an immense sorrow, and weeping. They could not at first distinguish very well who the strange person was, since they could only glimpse her through the bright light, but they did observe a woman who sat weeping. All the time that she spoke to them she wept. This is one of the details of the Apparition which Melanie noticed with particular care. Maximin also knew that the Blessed Virgin was weeping, though he did not see her tears. The tears of the Divine Mother flowed more freely and her face grew sadder when she spoke of the diverse calamities with which she threatened the earth; nevertheless Melanie remarked that even then the voice of the Beautiful Lady was not altered.

In his recital of the Apparition, Maximin makes no particular mention of the Blessed Virgin's tears, because the bright light which rather dimmed his view of her countenance prevented him from seeing her tears. However, he knew that she was sad and that she wept. This he strongly surmised from her sorrowful attitude at the moment she appeared and from the sound of her voice, which, though perfectly sweet, harmonious, rich and clear, bespoke deep sadness and indicated a flow of tears from the eyes of this good Mother.

The mysterious and holy tears of the Blessed Virgin did not fall to the ground nor even upon her raiment. These glistening teardrops fell down almost to the level of her knees, there breaking up into glittering particles and disappearing into tiny, starry spheres. The brilliant particles seemed to dissolve into a thick and luminous incense cloud, which, upon rising, melted into the vivid light around the person of the Blessed Virgin, and thus vanished among myriad rays of flame.

The tears of the Blessed Mother flowed in great abundance in a steady stream during all the time of her conversation with the children. This extraordinary weeping was accompanied by none of the convulsive sobs associated with the weeping of persons overwhelmed with grief. The features of our Weeping Mother remained perfectly regular and ravishing, in spite of the great sadness which they reflected.

Our Lady's Discourse

Melanie: *She said to us: "If my people will not submit, I shall be forced to let go the arm of my Son. It is so strong, so heavy, that I can no longer withhold it. For how long a time do I suffer for you! If I would not have my Son abandon you, I am compelled to pray to Him without ceasing, and as to you, you take no heed of it."*

In the children's recital of the discourse of Our Blessed Mother, we observe a few slight variations; for instance, in the opening sentence, Melanie uses the word "hand" where Maximin says "arm," each term being quite equivalent in meaning. The two witnesses almost always repeated the words of the Blessed Virgin exactly as they heard them spoken.

We must not presume, however, that their memory was at all times so prodigiously faultless that they did not occasionally, even on the same day, change a word at random or replace it by another having the same meaning. Such accidental alterations could be traced to a passing distraction or to fatigue brought about by the frequent repetition of the recitals.

Yet even this tendency to introduce unimportant changes was not ascertained for the period immediately following the day of the Apparition. It was simply noted that once in a while, especially after frequent reiteration of the recital, they abridged the report somewhat, Maximin the more so, since he omitted certain details, or suggested them in a few words and even epitomized parts of the discourse. For this reason, certain people made the objection that the two shepherds did not always report the same thing. The fact remains that the children adhered quite strictly to the substance of their narrative, though they sometimes abbreviated certain parts for the sake of convenience. On the other hand, it has been proved that people who took down the children's recitals in writing did not always put down exactly what they heard the children say. It is much less surprising that those who wrote the report from memory made alterations of their own; and the variations thus recorded are not to be attributed to the children.

Melanie: *Maximin had a mind to tell her to be silent and not to weep any more – that we were to give her help; but he didn't say anything because she kept right on speaking.*

Maximin: *I wanted to tell her to be quiet and to cease weeping – that I would bring her help.*

When the children first saw the Blessed Virgin seated upon the stones, Maximin thought it was a woman who had come to take away their lunch; that is to say, what remained of their light provisions. When they heard her speak of "the strong arm" of her Son and saw her weep, Melanie thought it was a poor woman of the neighborhood whose husband had threatened to beat her severely or had menaced, perhaps, to put her children to death. Maximin thought it was an unfortunate mother who had been beaten by a wicked son.

The boy was moved to compassion at her sad lot, and he had a mind to offer her comfort and protection. This puny lad of eleven would defend her against the fury of her son or her husband. These surmises on the part of the children show their natural reaction at the display of human sorrow.

Maximin was naturally affectionate, tender and compassionate; Melanie was somewhat less so. It is not surprising that the fine sentiment of charity which surged in the mind of the shepherd boy was not similarly manifested by Melanie. Maximin was of a sanguine disposition while Melanie was of a melancholic temperament.

Melanie: *And she said to us: "However much you pray, however much you do, you will never recompense the pains I have taken for you."*

In all the relations of the Apparition except one, the words cited above are to be found only in Melanie's recital and never in that of Maximin. It would seem that the lad very seldom repeated these words. Nevertheless they are recorded in Maximin's recital to Father Lagier; that is why there should be no hesitancy in accepting them as authentic.

As a matter of fact, Father Lagier, by himself alone, carries more authority in this particular than all other reporters taken together. His report was written under the most favorable conditions for perfect accuracy. He was himself a native of Corps. He understood the children's patois, or local dialect, thoroughly. He wrote his notes only four months and a half after the day of the Apparition.

He was not a believer in the extraordinary event at the time he made his personal investigation. He therefore took great pains to find fault with the children, and he wrote down exactly what they said in an attempt to snare them into contradictions, one against the other or each against himself.

He spared no time in his cross-examination, having little else to do just then except to visit and comfort his sick father at Corps. He pursued his inquiry at the season of the year when the children were no longer assailed by the thousands of demands of pilgrims, since the bad weather prevented the intrusion of visitors. Thus the children were more at liberty to answer with care and precision the questions and objections of Father Lagier.

The Cause of Her Grief

"Six days have I given you to labor, the seventh I have kept for myself, and they will not give it to me. It is this which makes the arm of my Son so heavy. Those who drive the carts cannot swear without introducing the name of my Son. These are the two things which make the arm of my Son so heavy."

Some narratives, generally the least important, read as follows: "My Son has given you six days...," or again, 'He (my Son) has given you six days to labor." That is not the accurate report of the Blessed Virgin's words as recited by the children, and they themselves often protested against those who spoke and wrote thus. "There are priests," said Melanie in 1847, "who come to question us and they write down what I say; then they say, 'It is not possible that the Blessed Virgin should have spoken thus' – and so they put down what they please. It is all the same to me; I let them do so, but I myself speak as I have heard."

Many persons have overwhelmed the two shepherds with objections on this score, saying that it was not the Blessed Virgin who had spoken to them, since surely she would not have adopted this kind of language. These people simply made manifest their ignorance of sacred Scripture, or their lack of faith in the Apparition and sometimes in the truths of the Gospel.

Other persons even dared to change the text of the children's recitals and put down "My Son has given you six days to labor," or "If the people will not submit" instead of "If my people will not submit." There is no absolute certainty that Maximin did not sometimes say "If the people" and "My Son has given you," since he was rather inclined to abridge his recital when time weighed heavily upon him. He could easily alter insignificant details and occasionally paraphrase parts of the discourse. However, when wishing to be brief, he generally omitted parts of the discourse rather than change the wording. Except on very rare occasions, and for brevity's sake, the children constantly adhered to the original wording of Our Lady's discourse.

One narrative gives the following wording: "I have given them (men, no doubt) six days to labor, says He, and the seventh, I have kept for Myself, and I cannot obtain it." This manner of reporting presumes that the Blessed Virgin wished to indicate that the words she cited were her Son's and not her own. This is contrary to all the most complete and accurate reports made of the children's recitals. Most handwritten narratives containing similar inaccuracies are dated in the year 1846.

The Blessed Virgin, while speaking directly, spoke nevertheless in the Name of God. The prophets of old often spoke in this peculiar fashion. Now if these humans could adopt this direct manner of speech, how much more reasonably ought we to accept the same form of address on the part of the Blessed Virgin, whom we acclaim as the Queen of Prophets. The expression "six days have I given you to labor" is far more forceful and impressive than the indirect phrasing, "My Son has given you."

Mary recalled the Law of God regarding the observance of the Sabbath, thus indicating that just as the Jews were obliged to sanctify the Sabbath, so are we Christians bound to observe the Law of the Church regarding Sunday. By these words the Blessed Virgin reproves, forbids and condemns servile work on the Lord's Day, and she imperiously demands the sanctifying of the Christian Sabbath. The profanation of the Lord's Day being the source of countless evils inflames the ire of God toward sinful humankind.

"Those who drive the carts..." At first thought, one may ask why, in condemning swearing, the Blessed Virgin singled out teamsters for her scathing rebuke. She did so primarily because in all countries this class of people is rather commonly addicted to this bad practice. Then, also, at the time of the Apparition, teamsters traveled the main road through Corps in larger numbers than in our own times (1863). Since the time of the Apparition this traffic has been largely diverted due to the construction of the Lyons-Marseilles Railway. Thus, the two shepherds, Melanie and Maximin, must have frequently met with these men when going through the town of Corps, particularly when climbing the steep hill at the entry of the town, where certain teamsters more than matched their speed with profanity. The children's familiarity with this class of delinquents explains why the Blessed Virgin aimed her stern reproof in their direction.

"(They) cannot swear without introducing the name of my Son." The word "swear" in this instance covers, besides blasphemy, all gross slang, uncouth and evil-sounding expletives such as are often heard in the conversations of ill-bred folk, especially in the lowest ranks of society and among the peasant class in general. The Blessed Virgin alludes to the total lack of restraint which accentuates the loss of temper on all occasions. She particularly condemns the free and unconsidered habit of mingling the Holy Name amidst vulgar outbursts of language under the slightest pretext or provocation. Incidentally, she also stresses very plainly that she is the Mother of God, since to blaspheme the Holy Name of God is to utter blasphemy against her Divine Son.

"These are the two things which make the arm of my Son so heavy." Sunday work and blasphemy are the two great evils which provoke Heaven's wrath and vengeance; in other words, these two grievances are the chief causes of Mary's tears at La Salette.

MERCIFUL WARNINGS

"If the harvest is spoilt, it is all on your account. I gave you warning last year in the potatoes, but you did not heed it. On the contrary, when you found the potatoes spoilt, you swore, you took the name of my Son in vain. They will continue to decay, so that by

Christmas there will be none left."

"If the harvest is spoilt..." The word "harvest" may be taken in the sense of all sorts of crops, but particularly the potato crops which were considerably damaged at Corps in 1846. "Last year" – that is, 1845 – since already, the year previous, the potato crops had suffered severe ruin in many of the surrounding localities. Instead of humbling themselves before God and recognizing in the spoiled crops a chastisement from above, certain farmers, upon digging up decayed potatoes in their fields, gave vent to their anger by means of horrible blasphemies.

"They will continue to decay so that by Christmas there will be none left." It is related that when the Blessed Virgin made this threat and prophecy, the boy Maximin felt deeply grieved to hear that the potatoes, which were at the time the main staple of the inhabitants of the mountains, and especially of his own folks at home, would continue to decay till none were left. "Oh, not so, Madam," he interjected. "The potatoes won't all go; we will surely yet find a few."

The Blessed Virgin foretold that so great would become the scarcity of potatoes that by Christmas of that year there would be hardly any available for consumption. As a matter of record, by Christmas there could not be found any potatoes to eat at Corps and the surrounding localities. The inhabitants could scarcely save a very small provision for planting in the spring.

On December 2, 1846, the Curé of Corps wrote to the Bishop of Grenoble concerning the poor of his parish. The cost of living for his parishioners had skyrocketed. Not one sack of potatoes had appeared on the market, and he himself had been unable to purchase any for his own use at any price whatsoever. Thus already, in 1846, the potatoes were decaying in an unusual manner.

The Blessed Virgin had announced that the terrible disease would continue with growing intensity. It has been verified that in 1846 there were hardly any potatoes unaffected by disease in France, in

Germany, in England, and especially in Ireland; hence the great suffering which many of the common people endured, particularly in Ireland. The terrible threat which the Blessed Virgin pronounced concerning the potatoes continued finding its fulfillment almost every year after 1846. Everybody sees it with his own eyes (1863).

Be it said, however, that the people of Corps and the environs turned to early profit the warnings of the Blessed Virgin, and were converted in a body in 1846 and 1847. It is true that they have already (1863) fallen off somewhat from their first fervor, but there still remain among them noticeable marks of sincere conversion. Since that period, also, these localities have enjoyed every year good and often very abundant harvests in wheat, grapes, potatoes and forage. Potatoes sometimes suffered decay again, after 1846, but only in small quantity. All these good people recognized the fact that they were well protected by Our Lady of La Salette. Let it also be noted that they honor that good Mother with great devotion. This they manifest in the beautiful and numerous processions which all these parishes organize each year to the Holy Mountain.

Melanie: *And now I did not understand what she wanted to say; I did not know what she meant by "pommes-de-terre" (potatoes). While she was saying, 'By Christmas there will be none left,' I was about to ask Maximin if he knew what "pommes-de-terre" meant. I was ready to ask him when at once the Lady said, "Ah, my children, you do not understand; I shall say it in a different way."*

Maximin: *Melanie did not understand very well and she began to ask me what it meant. Immediately, the Lady answered, "Ah, my children, you do not understand; I shall say it in a different way." And she spoke to us in patois.*

Thus far, Melanie had understood something of what the Blessed Virgin had said, but when she mentioned *pommes-de-terre (potatoes),* the girl was at a loss to grasp what was meant. It is hard

— 45 —

to see how the child had been able to follow everything the Lady had said, since all she had heard was spoken in French, unless the Blessed Mother had given her some slight measure of comprehension. Very likely she understood only a few words of all the Blessed Virgin uttered in French, but she did not grasp the full sense conveyed.

Melanie had never spoken anything but the dialect, or patois, of her region. She had never gone to school. She was unable to speak French. She did not even understand French except a few very simple words. This is easily explained when we note that the language usually spoken in these mountains is the patois, or local dialect, and that, previous to the time of the Apparition, French was hardly ever spoken even at Corps, the county seat.

To this day (1863), even the educated folk who know and speak French well, make it a point to speak the local dialect in their relations with the inhabitants of the region. At the time of the Apparition, even as today, there were people at Corps who spoke French fluently, but as a rule they did not use that language as the common medium of expression.

Since the day of the Apparition, the great inflow of pilgrims from all parts of France has contributed an incentive for the people of Corps to learn a little French. However, these country folk do not speak the language among themselves, only with outsiders. It should not surprise us that Melanie and Maximin could not speak or understand French, especially Melanie, who had lived five years in country places where not a single word of French was ever heard spoken.

Previous to the Apparition, Melanie and Maximin spoke and understood only the patois of their district – this is incontestable; however, since they had certainly heard some French spoken at Corps, which was a crossroad of passenger and truck traffic, it is almost equally certain that the children, especially Maximin, had picked up a scant vocabulary of French words. Yet this does not prove that they could express themselves in French in such a way as to be properly understood.

After the Apparition, Melanie's master remarked that the girl had a singular facility in expressing herself on all that concerned the great event. Immediately, she revealed her ability to give in French a few replies to the questions addressed to her in that tongue, although she had not been able to speak the language before. Little by little, after the Apparition, she began to speak French, very poorly, indeed, but, all in all, well enough to make herself understood by the pilgrims.

This, however, cannot properly be considered a miracle; first, because it is not sure that this girl would not have spoken a few words of French before the Apparition if she had been obliged to, as she was later, to answer questions put to her in that tongue; second, because even after the celestial vision she did not understand much French and spoke it very poorly; third, because only little by little did she and the boy, Maximin, acquire sufficient fluency in French.

However, considering their complete ignorance and their phenomenal incapacity in every respect, we may presume that the Blessed Virgin gave them a particular grace to help them express themselves somewhat in French, in order that they might be able to communicate to her people the message she had charged them to make known. Thus not only were they enabled to repeat in French that part of the discourse spoken in that language, but also to understand the questions addressed to them in French and to answer them in a satisfactory manner.

The truly great miracle relating to the children's knowledge of French is that the two lowly shepherds were able to retain, word for word, without quite understanding it all, that portion of the discourse which the Blessed Virgin delivered to them in French at one single and rapid utterance. This remarkable feat of memory was the first prodigy – and one of the greatest – wrought by Our Lady of La Salette in favor of the two witnesses. The people of Corps and visitors from distant places who have seen and heard and examined these children in the early days that followed the wonderful event were unanimous on this score.

When Melanie heard the Beautiful Lady speak of *pommes-de-terre (potatoes)*, she had a mind to turn toward Maximin and ask him what that meant in patois. At first, we do not see why she wanted to obtain this information from Maximin, since he was much younger than herself and just as ignorant as she was. However, she presumed that he was more apt than herself to understand French, since she had lived for the past five years in localities where not a word of French was spoken in any circumstance, while she knew that at Corps, where Maximin lived, people occasionally spoke French.

Since the lad had never been away from Corps, she supposed that he might know what *pommes-de-terre* signified. Abbé Arbaud wrote, in 1847, that the boy, Maximin, was a rather frequent intruder at the Café Magneau, situated next to his father's house. He went there not because it was a café but because it was the neighbor's place. Now many French-speaking customers frequented the Café Magneau. By dint of hearing and mere curiosity Maximin had come to learn a few words of French and even to use a few.

When Melanie was about to ask the boy what the strange words meant, she was prevented from putting the question to him and she kept her thought to herself. She had perhaps turned toward her companion, but the Beautiful Lady gave her no time to ask him, since she read the child's mind and deliberately changed from French into the patois of the region.

"Ah, my children, you do not understand." The Blessed Virgin spoke these words with great kindness and eagerness, as if she wished to offer an excuse for having used a language which they did not understand. Well did she know that they could hardly grasp all she said, but she had a reason for speaking first in French and then in the country dialect.

It did not really matter so very much whether the children fully understood what she said, since the discourse was not intended merely for their personal benefit. The witnesses were but the instruments and the channels, as it were, whereby her message could be transmitted to her people. The Queen of Heaven might have spoken in any language that suited her purpose.

Fr. Lagier meets with Maximin and Melanie

THE PATOIS OF CORPS

When the Beautiful Lady began to speak in patois she repeated that part of her discourse where mention is made of the potato crops, and she pursued her trend of thought without further ado. The patois which she spoke was that of Corps. It is a dialect spoken in that district only. The patois used in the surrounding regions resembles it in substance but differs considerably in pronunciation and vocabulary. The dialect of the nearby village of La Salette is noticeably different in many ways from that of Corps. It is not so light on the tongue but it is easier to write.

The patois of Corps belongs to a species of corrupt Provençal. With the gradual infiltration of French words, the dialect goes on deteriorating, with time. Outsiders find its pronunciation difficult, and as there are no set rules for its orthography very few can write it well. Even the people of the district do not write it with uniformity. The author (in his historical work, *The Abbé Jots it Down*) has striven to write it down exactly as it is pronounced. This patois, when well spoken, is sweet and harmonious to the ear. The Queen of Heaven spoke it as correctly and with as pure an accent as might be expected from the natives of the locality.

Certain know-its-alls have held that it could not be the Blessed Virgin who appeared at La Salette for the simple reason that the Mother of God would never lower herself to the necessity of using a jargon like the dialect of Corps. Nevertheless we maintain that the patois of Corps is as dignified a form of speech as any other vehicle of human expression. Before God, it enjoys as fair and noble a standing as any other language spoken among men.

True, being a local dialect it lacks the wider favor of the main languages of the civilized world, such as French, Italian, German and English. The Blessed Virgin could very easily have used any of these modern languages while enabling the children to understand all she said.

Evidently she had reasons of convenience in following the course she adopted. By speaking first in French and then in patois, she refuted beforehand a puerile and impertinent objection made by certain skeptics who pretended that it was not the Queen of Heaven who appeared on the Holy Mountain, but rather some intriguing, crafty woman of the locality, who skillfully showed herself to the children and promptly vanished before their astonished eyes.

Now, by speaking French, the Blessed Virgin proved that she was not a person of the locality since the few people in Corps who could speak French could be readily identified. Then, by speaking the local dialect, she proved that she was no stranger, since the patois which she spoke is used only at Corps. If she was not a person of the locality nor a stranger, whence then was she?

"If you have wheat, it is not good to sow it; all that you sow the insects will eat. What comes up will fall into dust when you thresh it."

This is how the farmers thresh wheat at Corps. At harvest time the corn is gathered in small sheaves, each sheaf containing a large handful of ears. Threshing is done by knocking the sheaves, one by one, against a stone until the grains of wheat are nearly all taken out. This operation is known as "knocking the corn." To get the rest of the grain out of the sheaves, each sheaf is taken in the left hand, laid on the knee, and then beaten with a small stick; or else the sheaves are untied, spread upon the threshing floor, and finished off with a flail. The finishing process is known as "pricking the corn."

"If you have wheat it is not good to sow it..." These words did not formulate a counsel, much less a command, on the part of the Blessed Virgin. No one has ever taken the statement in that sense, and the farmers of the district have gone right on sowing wheat each year just as they did before the Apparition. The expression must be understood as a Biblical idiom of great energy which the Divine Mother employed to warn of danger or ruined harvests.

The twofold scourge regarding the wheat threatened both the growing plant and the ripened ear of corn. What the insects left untouched would be found spoiled and would turn into dust at threshing. For several years after the Apparition, it was observed in certain localities that the wheat did almost literally fall into dust at threshing, or, at least, so little grain did it yield, that it seemed to melt under the flail. The ears of corn, which at first appeared fair and full, produced but few grains of wheat.

We may add that unto this day (1863), thanks be to God, this frightful menace relating to ruined wheat has been only partially fulfilled. But many a time the crops have been bad enough to open the eyes of those who saw the avenging hand of God in the plagues which have fallen upon us in the past ten or twenty years. The threats pronounced by Our Lady of La Salette concerning wheat and famine so alarmed the French Government, in 1846, that civil authorities wrote to the Bishop of Grenoble complaining that such rumors had been launched from his diocese.

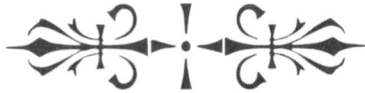

"There will come a great famine. Before the famine comes, the children under seven years of age will be seized with trembling and will die in the arms of those who hold them; and others will do penance by the famine."

"There will come a great famine…" The Blessed Virgin did not determine the time and place of the famine. This terrible threat may yet be fulfilled at any time. During several years after the Apparition, the crops have been very bad in France and several times a famine crisis seemed imminent.

"The children… will die…" During the years immediately following the Apparition of La Salette, a great number of children died from the effects of a strange epidemic. Many persons saw in this high rate of child mortality the accomplishment of the Blessed Virgin's threat. However, the mortality of the little children as depicted in the prophetic menaces of La Salette has not yet occurred. As there is no set time designated, it may yet happen.

"Others will do penance by the famine." The grown-ups, those above seven years of age, will suffer or die of hunger. Already in France, since 1846, a great number of people have perished from the effects of hunger caused by the exceedingly high cost of living. Nevertheless, the prophecy made by our Lady of La Salette, has, most fortunately, not yet been realized (1863). It may yet have its effect since we are not told when it shall happen.

"The walnuts will become worm-eaten." The expression "worm-eaten" renders the exact meaning of the patois, *boffas*. This patois idiom signifies the condition of walnuts that have been bored to the core and devoured by the enclosed worm. For several years after the Apparition, the walnut crops were of very meager quality in many districts of France, especially in the department of Isère, so rich in walnut trees.

"The grapes will rot." Since 1851, when the dread disease of the vines began to develop, this prophecy has been literally fulfilled more than once, in a great number of localities in France, in Italy, and almost all of Europe, in Asia and Africa. Before the appearance of the disease, the price of wine in France was from eight to fifteen francs per hectoliter. For the past twelve years (previous to 1863) wine sold at forty to sixty francs. Since 1851, this vineyard plague has been scientifically ascertained and its phenomenal spread seems but the literal fulfillment of the prophecy, "the grapes will rot." No one in the world can question this verified fact.

The prophecies concerning the potatoes and the grapes have, to this day (1863), been fulfilled to the letter in almost all countries. Those relating to the wheat, the mortality of children and the famine, have been but partially fulfilled; enough, however, to open the eyes of those who are not blinded by prejudice. Unfortunately, the three last scourges mentioned may yet be inflicted upon us.

Like a tender mother, Divine Providence first strives to bring people back to God by afflicting them with lesser evils, reserving more terrible scourges for a later date, in such a way as to spare people even while punishing them in the guise of timely warnings. It is evident that the loss of potatoes and of grapes is a lesser evil than famine and the plague.

All these threats of Our Lady of La Salette are of a conditional nature, and they were to be accomplished only if people refused to be converted. If people had turned back to God, these menaces would have remained unrealized. Even so, they would have lost none of their supernatural value.

The threats uttered by Jonah against Nineveh (Jonah 3:4) never came to be because by doing penance the Ninevites prevented their being fulfilled. The words of Jonah were nevertheless inspired from above. We may even remark that the prophecies of Jonah were not expressed in a conditional form as were those of La Salette. Jonah said in absolute terms: "Forty days more and Nineveh shall be overthrown...." Yet the Ninevites understood that these threats could be revoked by the will of God on condition that they did penance. If such absolute prophecies failed to materialize, how much more reasonably may we expect that the conditional prophecies of La Salette may never be brought to strict fulfillment.

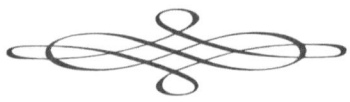

Secrets

Melanie: *Here the Lady kept silence for a moment. It seemed to me that she was speaking to Maximin, but I heard nothing. Then she told me a secret in French. In the meantime, Maximin amused himself with his shepherd-stick, driving at small stones which sometimes rolled down toward the Lady. I also held my stick in my hand.*

Maximin: *After that the Lady told me something in French, saying to me, "You will not tell this – nor this – nor this..." Then she kept silence for a moment and during that time I amused myself with my shepherd-stick. Then she continued in patois.*

It is interesting to note that during the first few months which followed the Apparition, the children said nothing more about their secrets. Thus it was generally believed, at least among the people of the district, that the secret matters which the Beautiful Lady had confided to the children concerned them alone personally, and consisted chiefly of certain counsels to help them lead a good life. That is why, in some of the least reliable reports, the children's secrets were called wise counsels or personal matters. This was altogether false, because even though their secrets are as little known today (1863) as they were in 1846, it is practically certain that they did not pertain to the children personally.

The Blessed Virgin gave a secret to each of the children, to Maximin first, then to Melanie, in French. While she spoke to the one, the other heard nothing, though the two children stood side by side and though she spoke in the same tone of voice as previously. It happened that, of a sudden, Melanie ceased hearing the words of the Beautiful Lady, though she could see her lips moving; then in turn the boy, Maximin, could hear her no longer, though it seemed to him that she kept on talking. During each interval of apparent silence, the two witnesses concluded that she had ceased speaking.

After the Apparition, the two shepherds asked each other what the Beautiful Lady was doing when she said nothing and only moved her lips. Then, each in turn, they told how, while she seemed to say nothing, she communicated to each something in particular, saying, "You will not tell this – nor this – nor this..." This is how they came to learn that they were each the possessor of a special secret.

While the Blessed Virgin confided the secret to Melanie, time seemed to weigh heavily on the boy, Maximin. However, he stayed where he was and whiled away the interval by twirling his cap on the end of his shepherd stick or knocking the pebbles at his feet with the sharp end of his staff. It is during this interval that he behaved most poorly in the presence of the Beautiful Lady, but he dared not utter a word.

Melanie and Maximin have never known each other's secret. It seems, however, that Melanie's secret was longer than that of Maximin. It is not positively known whether the secrets were quite different or substantially one and the same, that of Melanie being considerably more detailed. From the very beginning it has always been supposed that the secrets were different. The attitude of the Sovereign Pontiff and the few words he spoke while reading them, have confirmed this surmise.

In July, 1851, at the request of the Holy Father, Pope Pius IX, the two children communicated their secrets to Rome, in writing.

The two secrets put together must be at least as long as the whole known discourse of Our Lady of La Salette. Judging by their place in the recitals and by their immediate context, they presumably contained threats similar to those found in the words preceding their utterance. The Blessed Virgin confided the secrets after speaking of spoiled wheat, famine, infant mortality, walnut blight and the grape disease.

After delivering the secrets she said, "If they are converted," and so on. Now the conversion she had in mind seems to have been the indispensable condition for the prevention not only of the evils she foretold to the two witnesses, but likewise of the calamities she revealed to each in particular; otherwise she would not have inserted the secrets at this juncture of the discourse.

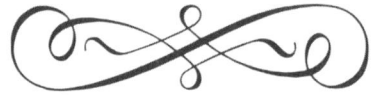

Melanie: *Then she said: "If they are converted, the stones and the rocks will be changed into heaps of wheat, and the potatoes will be self-sown in the fields."*

"If they are converted..." Sincere and general conversion, at least among the majority of the people, is the indispensable condition whereby the occurrence of the threatened evils may be forestalled.

"Heaps of wheat." The patois term, *mountseous*, translated 'heaps,' signifies literally 'mounds' and by extension "huge heaps." "Heaps of wheat" is a Biblical hyperbole employed by the Blessed Virgin to signify extraordinary fertility or exceeding abundance.

"The potatoes will be self-sown in the fields." Again with a slight exaggeration peculiar to scriptural language, the expression signifies that the potatoes will be found self-sown in the ground, so that there will be no need of sowing them.

Maximin: *And then she said to us: "Do you say your prayers well, my children?" We told her, all two together, "O no, Madam, not very well." And then she said to us: "Ah, my children, you must be sure to say them well, morning and evening; when you cannot do better say at least an Our Father and a Hail Mary. But when you have time, say more."*

"Do you say your prayers well?" – that is, regularly, punctually, every day, each morning and evening.

"Not very well" – that is, rarely, if ever, and poorly at that.

"You must be sure to say them well." Never omit them and say them devoutly.

"Morning and evening." In the patois of Corps, the expression is peculiarly inverted, *vepre et mati – eve and morn*. It is similar to the Biblical term, "Evening came and morning followed..." (Genesis 1:5).

"When you have time..." When it is really impossible to say long prayers or even the common form of evening and morning prayers, "say at least a *Pater* and an *Ave Maria*," rather than omit your prayers entirely. This does not mean that an *Our Father* and a *Hail Mary* will always do for morning and evening prayer, but in exceptional cases the short prayer will cover the obligation. The Blessed Virgin was here addressing two poor ignorant children who hardly knew the *Our Father* and the *Hail Mary*. She could not very well exact longer prayers.

COMPLAINTS

"There are none who go to Mass but a few aged women, the rest work on a Sunday all the summer; and in the winter, when they know not what to do, they go to Mass only to mock at religion. During Lent they go to the butcher shop like dogs."

Unfortunately, this was only too true of the town of Corps and of the surrounding regions at the time of the Apparition. Since then, however, conditions are quite different, though the people of Corps and the outlying districts are not as thoroughly converted as might be expected after the heavenly intervention of La Salette.

In the summertime, people worked regularly on Sunday or sought frivolous amusements, but they seldom if ever went to Mass. They gave the Sabbath over to dancing, or what was considered such in the region. At Corps and the environs, dancing was a general passion, a sort of feverish frenzy that seized upon one and all. After the Apparition, this practice fell off entirely. Except for the fact that the two children simply narrated what they saw and heard on the Holy Mountain, there was no organized crusade against dancing as a disreputable form of recreation. As a result of the children's words, forbidden work also ceased entirely on Sunday.

In this part of her discourse, the Blessed Virgin reproved her people for missing Mass and she condemned anew the evil of Sunday work, a crime so grievous that she attacked it directly in as many as four instances, whereas she condemned blasphemy twice, and other evils only once. Outside a few aged women, practically all the others – men, women, old folks and children – scrupled not at all to miss Sunday Mass all through the fair season.

"In winter when they know not what to do..." The inhabitants of this mountain district found little to do after All Saints' Day, when work in the fields had ceased and bad weather, cold and snow confined them to home chores. They then considered going to Mass on Sunday as a proper diversion of a social nature.

"Only to mock at religion." Their behavior at church savored more of irreligion than of piety. However, they could not be accused of outright and systematic impiety or hatred of religion. They did lack seriousness, chattered irreverently in the holy place, displayed mundane dress and showed but few marks of attention and recollection during the Holy Sacrifice of the Mass.

Incidentally, it is reported that certain boys of the parish of Corps had the habit of carrying pebbles in their pockets to throw at the girls in order to make them turn around during the sermon or the ceremonies of the Mass, and otherwise annoy them in a spirit of uncouth and rustic humor. This abuse, if not a frequent occurrence, was nevertheless a serious disorder. That is why two or three of the first relations of the Apparition state: "The boys, when they know not what to do, go to church to mock at religion; they fill their pockets with pebbles to throw them afterwards at the girls."

Of course, the Blessed Virgin did not say these words. Maximin, at the instigation of a few persons of Corps whom this abuse afflicted a great deal, sometimes inserted the words in his early recitals, but soon he ceased doing so. However, that did not stop the opponents of the Apparition from making a great noise on the subject. None of the abuses reproved by the Blessed Virgin exist any longer at Corps, since the Apparition. Mass is regularly attended and is devoutly heard.

"During Lent they go to the butcher shop like dogs." Besides Lent, some of the reports added Fridays and Saturdays. This was quite inexact. In their recitals, the children never specified any other time than Lent. No doubt the Blessed Virgin may have meant to indicate Fridays, Saturdays, Vigils and Ember Days while speaking of the penitential season, but she did not say so explicitly. "Like dogs" is rather a harsh expression from the lips of the Blessed Virgin, and it forcefully conveys the idea of avidity and voracity among sensual Christians whose behavior on days of fast and abstinence evokes the animal instincts of dogs that prowl around the market place or the butcher shops.

RUINED WHEAT

Melanie: *And then she said: "Have you never seen wheat that was spoilt, my children?" Maximin answered, "O no, Madam!" For me, I did not know to which of us she asked this question and I* *replied very gently, "No, Madam, I have never seen any yet."*

Maximin: *And then she said to us: "Have you not yet seen spoiled wheat, my children?" I answered, "O no, Madam, we have not seen any."*

Terre du Coin

(field of Coin or Corner Field)

The Blessed Virgin asked them if they had not seen spoilt wheat, very likely that year, 1846, at harvest time. Melanie did not know which of them she was addressing in particular, for the Beautiful Lady spoke to Maximin as well as to her, since she said, "My children." The little girl replied softly, almost in a low tone of voice. Maximin answered in the name of both.

Melanie had in fact never seen spoilt wheat. Maximin had seen some once out in the fields with his father, but he had completely forgotten the incident. The Blessed Virgin was about to recall it to his mind.

Maximin: *So she said to me: "But you, my child, you must surely have seen some, once when you were near the farm of Coin with your father."*

The Blessed Virgin now spoke to Maximin alone and brought back to his mind the time that he had seen spoiled wheat in a field near the hamlet of Coin, a little more than two miles west of the town of Corps. Coin (translated Corner) lies at the intersection of the River Drac and the brook which flows down from La Salette. Mr. Giraud, Maximin's father, was a wheelwright by trade. On the day referred to by the Blessed Virgin in her discourse, he had gone to the hamlet of Coin in order to purchase a tree trunk to supply the lumber needed at his carpentry work.

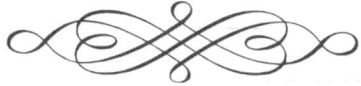

"The master of the field told your father to go and see his ruined wheat. You went both together. You took two or three of the ears into your hands, and rubbed them, and they fell all into dust; and then you returned home."

The master of the field, Mr. Armand, was a landowner of the hamlet of Coin, where Mr. Giraud, Maximin's father, went to buy new-cut timber. The proprietor of the farm took his customer to inspect a particular tree-trunk, and as they were discussing the year's harvest they came by a corn field. Mr. Armand interrupted the conversation and invited Mr. Giraud to go to see his ruined wheat. They made directly for the nearest corn patch and each in turn plucked two or three ears of corn and rubbed them in his hands. Maximin did likewise, for he could not forego doing what his elders did, otherwise we might have to presume that the lad had been handcuffed. He was not the kind of child to be satisfied with merely looking on.

Thus, as soon as they rubbed the ears of corn in the palm of their hands, they observed that the grains of wheat fell into dust. It is said that on seeing that, Maximin's father cried out, "O my God, what will we do this year if the wheat continues to decay like this?" It seems that the incident happened around early harvest time. When they shook and pressed the ears of corn in their hands, the grains of wheat did not drop out clean and hard, but rather they crumbled and fell into black dust.

"When you were still half an hour's distance from Corps, your father gave you a piece of bread, and said to you, 'Here, my child, eat some bread this year at least; I don't know who will eat any next year if the wheat goes on like that.'"

After purchasing the trunk of an ash tree, Mr. Giraud returned to Corps with the lad Maximin. The distance from the hamlet of Coin to the town of Corps is about one hour's walk. The incident here recorded took place at a point about halfway to Corps, where the road opens upon the plain west of the town. "Eat some bread this year at least," that is, 1846. "I know not who will eat any next year…," hence in 1847.

Melanie: *And then Maximin said to her, "Oh! yes, Madam, I recollect; just this moment I did not remember."*

Maximin: *And then I said to her, "That is very true, Madam, I did not remember it."*

These precise details given by the Blessed Virgin brought back to the boy's memory one of those thousands of circumstances of daily life which of themselves seem quite insignificant and are readily forgotten, especially by a child as lightheaded and distracted as was Maximin.

It is related that when Maximin returned to Corps, on Sunday, Sept. 20, he went to see his father, who was at a café in town, and told him that the day previous he had seen a Beautiful Lady. The father set him upon his knees and listened to him as he narrated the story of the Apparition. He was strongly impressed, especially by the incident of the ruined wheat, which no one could have known. Tears filled his eyes as he fixed his gaze on his child and with a gentle bit of profanity said to him: "There... you're too dense a child to have invented or learned such a tale." The boy's recital convinced him of the reality of the Apparition and converted him on the spot.

In his report, Abbé Chambon testifies to have met Maximin's father, who declared to him that the incident of the ruined wheat had strongly impressed him, since he had spoken of the occurrence to no one. The report has been confirmed that Maximin's father became a better Christian after the Apparition.

Writes Abbé Day, in his relation: "When the child narrated the event to his father, the latter shed tears at hearing the episode of the ruined wheat, which he recalled very well." Maximin's father died a few years after the Apparition.

It is likewise related that even though Maximin's father was vividly impressed by the recital of the Apparition and showed marks of sincere conversion on that occasion, yet for several months after the event it did not prevent him from handling the child rudely and at times brutally. And why so? Because the opponents of the Apparition kept dinning into his ears that he should stop the lad from telling his story, and that people at large complained a great deal about him for letting his child blabber this sort of story all around. The poor father became so bewildered with what he considered personal wrong that he sometimes gave way to fits of high temper and overwhelmed the lad with blows, trying to reduce him to silence and to cut short all this kind of publicity. However, this did not hinder the child from telling everybody what the Beautiful Lady had charged him to make known to all her people.

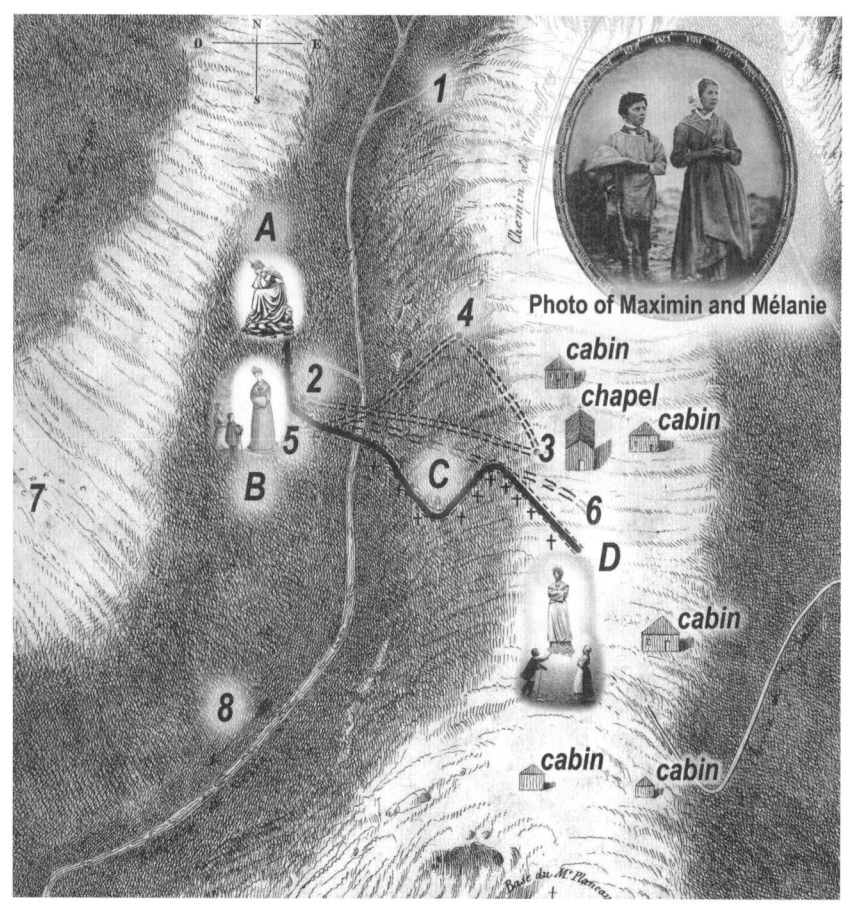

Photo of Maximin and Mélanie

Explanation of Site of
La Salette Apparition, Sept. 19, 1846:

Mary: **A:** *the miraculous fountain where Our Lady was seated, weeping;* **B:** *place of their conversation;* **C:** *path marked by crosses where Our Lady walked (130 feet);* **D:** *the place where Our Lady disappeared.*

Children: **1:** *the Men's Spring where the children ate;* **2:** *area where they fell asleep;* **3:** *the place where the children looked for their cows;* **4:** *place from where the children saw the globe of light;* **5:** *place of conversation and path the children took to top of knoll*

(5-6); **6:** *where children saw Our Lady disappear;* **7:** *the area where the cows were grazing;* **8:** *animal's fountain.*

chapel: *the provisional chapel;* **cabin:** *the five cabins built after the Apparition;* **Note:** *solid line indicates Our Lady's path; dotted lines indicate the children's path.*

Her Parting Words

Melanie: *After that the Lady said to us in French, "Well, my children, you will make this known to all my people."*

The Blessed Virgin ended her discourse as she had begun it, in French. It was also in French that she gave a private message to the children, although she spoke in patois, or local dialect, immediately before and after delivering the secrets. "Well, my children, you will make this known…" – as if she said, "Now then, my children, I charge you to make this message known, to broadcast far and wide all you have here seen and heard – my profound affliction, my tears, my complaints, my reproaches, my threats, my promises, all that concerns my person and my bearing." "To all my people": to everyone – man and woman, young and old, rich and poor, learned and ignorant, good or bad, great and small, priests and nuns, lay people and religious, the French, the English, the Italians, the Spaniards – to all Christians, to all nations, to the whole Catholic world, to all my people.

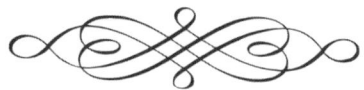

Melanie: *When she had ended these last words she turned suddenly and crossed the brook, then, without turning towards us, she said again in French, "Well, my children, you will make this known to all my people."*

Maximin: *Then she crossed the brook and when she was a few* *steps beyond the brook, she said to us once more, without turning towards us, "Well, my children, you will make this known to all my people."*

During the conversation the Blessed Virgin and the children stood forming a triangle; that is, Maximin was at the left, and Melanie was at the right, of the Beautiful Lady, but both stood exactly facing her. When she had finished her discourse she moved as if intent on going directly forward, but she turned around slightly to her left in order to avoid Maximin, who stood in her path on the margin of the brook. But as soon as he saw her advancing toward him, the boy stepped back toward Melanie, thus allowing the Queen of Heaven to proceed almost exactly to the spot where he had been standing during the conversation.

When Melanie saw the Beautiful Lady take a few steps downward and Maximin step back to let her pass, she turned to her right and stood elbowing her companion as before, but the two children were now facing east instead of directly north. The Blessed Virgin did not walk between them, but she passed right in front of them, close to Maximin. She took three or four steps alongside the brook, in a southern direction, and then crossed the dry bed of the brook, her feet gently touching a large stepping-stone which the shepherds of the region used when crossing the brook in time of flood.

This stone was carried away by pilgrims fifteen days after the Apparition. Another stone of similar size was later set in its place as a marker. It lies some twenty feet south of the miraculous fountain and about ten feet from the cross which marks the place of the conversation.

The Apparition and the Conversation took place on the right bank of the brook, and the Blessed Virgin crossed over to the left. Without turning back toward the children, who were still standing near the place of the conversation, about twelve feet behind her, she told them a second time, in French, "Well, my children, you will make this known to all my people." While saying these words she continued to walk in a southeastern direction. She repeated her parting words in the identical phrasing. Thus her last exhortation was spoken first on the right margin of the brook and reiterated about twenty feet on the left, across the brook.

"Well, my children, you will make this known to all my people." These were the last words the Blessed Virgin spoke in her Apparition. The rest of the time which she spent with the children she uttered not another word. After measuring mentally the length of the secret and comparing it with the length of the recital of our Lady's discourse, Melanie concluded that, all in all, the conversation, including the secrets, took approximately one-half hour. But for the two children the time of this mysterious colloquy sped by with the rapidity of lightning. When she ended her last words it seemed to them as if she had just begun to address them.

While the Blessed Virgin spoke to them, the two little shepherds felt as though her words were being deeply engraved and stereotyped on the tables of their treacherous memory, and this strong imprint was effected as soon as her words struck their ears, or rather their hearts, since they caught her words more with their hearts than with their ears, so that ever after they remembered them all and could never forget them.

Only once, and that somewhat rapidly, the Divine Mother told the children all that she charged them to transmit to her people, yet they retained all of it perfectly, the French as well as the dialect, whether or not they understood everything. Though this fact has received rather scant notice, it remains nevertheless one of the most signal prodigies connected with the Apparition; it alone might suffice to establish the supernatural origin of the great event of La Salette.

On the very evening of the day of the Apparition, without worrying whether they were listened to or not and despite all manner of threats and promises, the children began to fulfill their heavenly mission and to make known the teachings of the Beautiful Lady. From the very beginning, all sorts of objections were brought up against them. They were severely menaced and even rudely insulted but they could not be silenced. "We have received an order to tell everything" was their only rebuttal, and so they did.

Whether their questioners were learned or ignorant, great or small, rich or poor, men or women, priests or lay people, believers or unbelievers, pious or wicked, compatriots or strangers, it was of no concern to them. Without fear or favor, they told the same thing to one and all. They answered all questions without seeking to please or displease anyone, and with little regard to what people might think or say of them. We might say that never were ministers of the Gospel more independent or more faithful in accomplishing their mission. Never was the mere natural or human element less perceptible in the discharge of a supernatural task toward one's fellow human beings. These children seemed content to serve as the channels and instruments at the disposal of the one who told them, "Well, my children, you will make this known to all my people."

These two ignorant shepherds were never in the least embarrassed in answering all questions and refuting all objections put to them, no matter how subtle or how gross these attacks might appear. They were never disturbed or ruffled when told things that were absurd or painful or insulting to them, or when someone manifested incredulity in what they reported. With all simplicity, frankness, calmness, sweetness and energy they answered, "We are charged to tell you these things – not to make you believe them."

They never tired of repeating exactly the same things every day, sometimes as often as fifty or one hundred times a day. They seemed to experience no special trouble, nor pleasure either, in rehearsing them over and over again in the presence of all kinds of listeners. They did just what they were told to do, that is, make known to the people what they had seen and heard.

When we study the apostolic conduct of these children we discover in them the exemplars, as it were, of model preachers and catechists, and in certain respects even of confessors and of such as are charged to instruct others in their religious duties to combat prevalent abuses.

They never faltered in any difficult ordeal nor did they weaken before any opposition. Never once did they fail to meet the high standard required by their celestial mission. Never did they show signs of vanity at the wonderful things they uttered or at the stunning replies they delivered. They were indifferent to the enormous crowds of people who pressed around them from all classes of society and all countries – crowds ranging from five to forty thousand that listened to them with mute admiration. In the person of Maximin and of Melanie, Our Lady of La Salette seems to have left us models worth copying both in the manner of their announcing her message and in the doctrine that we are to teach to the world.

It has been observed that at the beginning Maximin showed less ease and facility than Melanie in reciting the Apparition and in replying to the questions of the crowds. This may explain why people questioned him more rarely than they did Melanie, yet, when giving information and in refuting objections, he was quite as alert and as capable as his young companion.

The Ascent of the Knoll

Maximin: *When she was through speaking she began to walk up the knoll slowly and quite close to us. First she passed in front of us.*

When she was through speaking, that is, after she had repeated the last words she spoke, "Well, my children, you will make this known to all my people," she was then on the other side of the brook while the children were still standing at the place of the Conversation. "She went up quite close to us" – that is, a few yards away from the place of the Apparition near which the children stood.

When the conversation was over, the Beautiful Lady crossed the brook, going from west to east, and ascended the hillock which rose before her. She walked slowly, no doubt in order that the two shepherds might be able to follow her without difficulty. She walked with the slow, ordinary step of a person going up hill.

Melanie: *Then she ascended the height as far as the spot where we had gone to look for our cows. We noticed that as she walked up, she did not set her feet on the ground but she moved along on the*  *tips of the grass without even bending it.*

Maximin: *She went up about fifteen steps walking on the grass as if she were suspended in the air. Her feet touched only the tips of the grass.*

"She went up about fifteen steps..." Measurements indicate that the whole distance covered was about eighteen yards, bird's flight, from the place where she spoke her last words up to the place of the Assumption, but as many as twenty-eight or twenty-nine yards retracing the course which she followed.

"As far as the spot where we had gone to look for the cows" – that is, the summit of the same hillock but not exactly on the same spot, since the place from which they had found their lost cattle was perhaps ten yards or so farther north from the place of the Blessed Virgin's Assumption.

"She moved along on the tips of the grass without even bending it." The mountain grass in that place was about five or six inches high.

"As if she were suspended in the air" – that is, since her feet were five or six inches above the ground they only grazed the tips of the grass. She moved her feet in the manner of a person walking, if people may be said to walk on air. Her body showed none of the movements which accompany the movement of the feet when a person walks.

She progressed very slowly and seemed rather to glide over the grass, being moved, as it were, by a strange and invisible force. That is why Maximin and Melanie said that the Beautiful Lady glided rather than walked – nevertheless while she seemed to glide her feet moved as if she were really walking. "She glided over the tips of the grass." When the children looked at the feet of the Blessed Virgin and saw them move away, they concluded that she was walking, but when they observed her motionless body, they had the impression that she simply glided over the blades of grass.

The feet of the Blessed Virgin touched the very tips of the grass but made it neither bend nor stir in the least. This shows that her weightless body was not an ordinary earthly and mortal frame, since all its weight could not so much as deflect a mere blade of grass. The chief kind of grazing on these mountains is a sort of wild hay, an extremely fine and billowing grass, which the flimsiest weight may bend and the lightest breeze agitate.

In her ascent to the summit of the hillock, the Blessed Virgin made no perceptible effort –she did not stoop forward, though she climbed a rather steep slope, an incline graded six inches to the yard, if we trace her original course.

Melanie: *We crossed the brook after her and followed her closely. As she ascended the mound ice walked very close to her, a step or*

two behind.

Maximin: *And we followed her very closely up to the very summit of the hillock. We spoke not a word to each other.*

The children remained at the place of the Conversation until the Blessed Virgin had already taken a few steps beyond the brook. They were watching her as she moved away from them when, of a sudden, hurrying across the brook, they overtook her and followed her to the top of the hillock.

They said that they followed her closely, that is, they were four or five feet away from her at either side, Melanie going a little forward to the left and Maximin somewhat behind, at the right of the Beautiful Lady. So captivated had the two shepherds been by the sweetness of her voice and the beauty of her person that they were unable to part from her and were impelled to follow in her footsteps wherever she might go, pursuing the very detours which she traced in her course.

They hardly noticed where they set their feet along the stony incline, being watchful only to follow the path she took. They climbed to the summit of the height southeast of the place of the Apparition, a few yards south of the spot where they had gone to look for their cows.

From the bottom of the ravine to the top of the slope where the Blessed Virgin ascended the distance is about twenty-eight yards in a straight line and some thirty-four or thirty-five yards along the path which she followed. The ravine was about fifteen feet in depth. The height on which the Blessed Virgin mounted and where she rose into the heavens was called the Collet (or Little Neck), a narrow stretch of ground between two ravines, east and west. The embankment raised for the construction of the Sanctuary has obliterated the Collet and the two ravines.

During all the time of the Apparition, from the moment Maximin told Melanie to pick up her shepherd-stick and not be afraid, the two children said not a word to each other; neither while running down to meet the Beautiful Lady nor all the while that she spoke to them. Likewise they stood silent when she moved away from them, ascended the knoll, and rose up in the air to disappear from view.

It seems that her august presence struck them mute. They looked on and moved about but always in the greatest silence, uttering not a word to each other and not even to the Beautiful Lady, except when she asked them a question, and in that case they answered simply and modestly.

Only when the Beautiful Lady had entirely disappeared and when the light around her had vanished completely did the two shepherds begin to speak to each other again. Until then they were too much absorbed with what they saw and heard to try to communicate with each other, although Melanie was once about to ask Maximin very softly what pommes-de-terre meant, which she did not understand.

On his part, Maximin was once about to speak to the Beautiful Lady to tell her that she should cease weeping and that he would like to help her, but he, too, refrained from talking. We may then apply to the entire duration of the Apparition what Maximin said of the moment they followed the Beautiful Lady up the knoll: "We said nothing to each other." They had no need of saying anything during the Celestial Vision – their sole occupation was to look on and listen in profound silence.

Melanie: *When she ascended the knoll, she set her feet on the ground as do people when they walk; we saw her feet move along.*

Maximin: *I saw her feet moving along.*

"She set her feet on the ground." By these words Melanie does not mean to say that the Blessed Virgin's feet really touched the ground, for they grazed only the tips of the grass and seemed suspended five or six inches in the air. Previously the child had said, "We noticed that when she walked she did not set her feet on the ground." At first reading there seems to be a contradiction in her words. But this contradiction is only apparent, since the girl speaks from different viewpoints. When Melanie says that they noticed that the Blessed Virgin did not set her feet on the ground, she meant that her feet appeared at the level of the tips of the glass and therefore did not touch the ground. When, on the contrary, she says that the Blessed Virgin set her feet on the ground, she wants us to understand that she moved her feet the same way any person does in the act of walking on firm ground.

To throw light on apparent contradictions which arise in the course of the children's recitals, one must always examine the context of the passage which contains the difficulty, and ascertain the exact idea which the witnesses wished to express. Thus it appears that the Blessed Virgin, as described by the children, unlike any mortal creature, seemed to walk and to glide in the air.

During her Apparition at La Salette, the Blessed Virgin walked twice; first, when she advanced from the place of the Apparition to the place of the Conversation; second, when she crossed the brook and ascended the elevation from which she arose and disappeared.

She walked gravely, with slow majesty, adapting her steps to those of the two little shepherds who followed her, so as not to tire them out or put them out of breath as they retraced her footsteps up the rude incline. "She walked softly," said the boy, Maximin.

When the Beautiful Lady descended from the place of the Apparition to that of the Conversation, the children did not observe whether her feet touched the ground or not; first, because amid the strong light which surrounded the Blessed Virgin they could not even clearly discern her august person; second, because as they stood quite a distance above her on the hillside, it was rather difficult for them just at that moment to see her feet. It seems, however, that during the whole time of the Apparition her feet never touched the ground. When she stood speaking to the children she was raised five or six inches above the ground, just as when she ascended the knoll. Just before she started to walk, the children did not remark that she suddenly rose to that height above the grass, therefore she must have been standing at that level all during her discourse. Most likely, too, she had not been really seated upon the stone bench at the moment of her appearing to the children; she simply seemed to be in that position. Moreover, in this particular, the children were unable to discern anything very clearly.

Melanie: *She ascended the knoll in silence and she made two slight detours before reaching the summit.*

The Beautiful Lady and the two children made the ascent of the knoll in silence. When the Blessed Virgin walked, she did so in silence. Thus she did not speak when she proceeded from the place of the Apparition to that of the Conversation, except for the last words of her invitation to the children: "Come near, my children, I am here to tell you great news." However, she was walking when she repeated the last injunction, "Well, my children, you will make this known to all my people." After these last words she kept absolute silence until she had entirely disappeared.

On the way up the knoll she made two slight detours, that is, she did not climb the mound in a straight line, probably because the two little shepherds might have found it difficult to follow her, seeing that the ascent was steep and stony. True, the two children, previous to the Apparition, had hurried up the knoll to look for their cows, but it was not befitting that they should make the same strenuous effort in following the footsteps of the good and merciful Mother. For anyone who climbs the site of the ascent, it is a comparatively easy task to retrace the course taken by Our Lady up the knoll of her Assumption.

One reason for the detours made by the Blessed Virgin to reach the summit of the elevation was perhaps the slippery condition of the slope. Moreover, there was a trodden path already marked out on the hillside for the shepherds of these mountains; it ran transversely from the summit down to the dry spring. This path the Blessed Virgin followed for a few yards after crossing the brook, then she abandoned it and took another similar path northward, running parallel with the first and leading from the summit of the knoll down to the Men's Spring. The children had taken this higher path on their way to eat their dinner at that spring.

Some people assert that at the time of the Apparition there was another small path that crossed these two in a perpendicular line. Thus the Blessed Virgin would have taken this crossway to go from the first to the second path already mentioned.

Melanie: *Now I passed in front of her and Maximin was a little aside of her, two or three steps away.*

Maximin: *Melanie passed in front of the Lady and I was at her side two or three steps away.*

After crossing the brook, Melanie did not follow the Blessed Virgin, but rather preceded her, that is, she climbed straight up and found herself in front of the Beautiful Lady, who, after taking a few steps in the southeasterly direction, returned toward the northeast. Melanie passed in front of her about midway between the place of the Conversation and that of the Assumption, that is, at a point some eleven yards from the summit of the knoll, bird's flight. In her ascent, Melanie did not exactly walk in front of the Blessed Virgin but slightly on her left, that is, she was about two steps ahead of the Beautiful Lady, and at her left side.

When the Blessed Virgin had nearly reached the summit of the knoll she began to rise from the ground. At that moment, Melanie set herself directly facing her, still two or three steps away, and she could contemplate her well at ease. Twice, then, did Melanie pass in front of the Blessed Virgin: first, toward the middle of the ascent, when, instead of following her as did Maximin, she passed ahead of her about two or three steps on her left, keeping this lead until she reached the top of the ridge; second, when she placed herself right in front of her as she rose in the air.

As soon as the Blessed Virgin uttered her last words beyond the brook, Melanie crossed over immediately, climbed straight up, and thus happened to be in front of her, that is, what she calls the first slight detour, because the Beautiful Lady had just made an elbow-turn in her progress, and instead of climbing on toward the southeast she now advanced toward the northeast. Thus while Melanie preceded the Blessed Virgin at the middle of the ascent, Maximin followed her step by step, keeping close on her right. The Blessed Virgin was therefore between the two children, Melanie a few steps ahead, on her right and Maximin a few steps behind her, on her left. Maximin stayed behind the Blessed Virgin simply because, instead of climbing up directly like his little companion, he pursued the path taken by the Beautiful Lady wherever she turned.

What naturally moved the little girl to pass in front of the Blessed Virgin was probably the fact that, having already been privileged to contemplate her ravishing features during the Conversation, she desired to view them again; whereas Maximin, not having been able to see her face quite clearly, did not feel urged to gaze upon it anew.

It is worthy of note that during the great event of the Apparition the little girl, Melanie, played a more remarkable role than did Maximin.

> 1) She was first to awake and then she roused her companion.

> 2) She was the first to climb the hillock to go in quest of the cows.

3) She was the first to come down after discovering the lost cattle.

4) She was the first to see the great light in the ravine and she pointed it out to Maximin.

5) She was the first to run down to the bed of the ravine when the Beautiful Lady told them to come near and not be afraid.

6) She was the first to reach the person of the Blessed Virgin and to stand right near her.

7) She alone had the signal privilege of seeing distinctly the face and tears of the Queen of Heaven and Earth.

8) She was the first to start in the footsteps of the Blessed Virgin when she began the ascent of the knoll.

9) She took the lead and passed in front of the Beautiful Lady during the ascent.

10) She alone stood facing the Beautiful Lady and contemplated her features when she arose in the air and until she had entirely disappeared.

11) It was Melanie who first surmised that "they had seen a great saint."

12) To the little girl, Mary confided the longer secret and apparently the more important one.

13) The girl Melanie always gave more abundant details in her description of the person of the Blessed Virgin.

The lad Maximin, on the other hand, played but a secondary role during the Apparition. This can be attributed to a special design of

Divine Providence and of the Blessed Virgin. One might invoke in this particular situation the natural effect of circumstance, seeing that Melanie was much older than Maximin and therefore more solicitous and more on the alert in all her movements. Nevertheless, if the Blessed Virgin had wanted the boy to play the first role, she would have overlooked his age or would have chosen an older boy to witness her Apparition.

Leaving aside the problematic aspect of the discussion, we may suggest that women should take to heart the fact of Melanie's preponderant role and conclude that theirs is a similar role to fulfill in the world as a consequence of the Apparition of Our Lady of La Salette.

The Assumption and Disappearance

Melanie: *Then, after a very brief pause, this Beautiful Lady began to rise a little more than three feet above the ground. She remained suspended a moment in the air. Then she gazed up toward heaven and down toward earth.*

Maximin: *Before disappearing, this Beautiful Lady rose up like this, a little more than three feet from the ground. She remained thus suspended in the air for a moment.*

Having arrived near the topmost point of the knoll, the Blessed Virgin halted a very brief instant, paused a while, as Melanie said, and then rose not quite four feet from the ground; that is, near the level of the children's heads, since they were of very small stature for their age. In fact, she rose much higher than the level of Maximin's head, since besides being small in stature he was then standing some three feet or more below, on the slope of the ravine. This explains why, when the Blessed Virgin had almost entirely disappeared, the lad jumped up and reached out with his hand to catch some of the roses that were around her feet. Had the boy been standing on the level from which the Blessed Virgin rose, he could easily have reached her feet by merely stretching out his hand.

She remained suspended in air a brief instant without uttering a word. During that pause she raised her eyes to heaven and then lowered them to earth, without glancing either right or left but looking straight ahead, facing the Italian skies toward Rome. Perhaps she was then addressing an ardent prayer to her Son in behalf of the center of the Catholic world and in behalf of its august Head, the Sovereign Pontiff.

It was no doubt with a special design that she rose and vanished from view, her face turned toward Rome, and that she cast a sad and suppliant look heavenward and then lowered her gaze to the earth in the direction of the Eternal City.

When the Blessed Virgin rose in the air, Melanie happened to be standing in front of her, but slightly at her left and about three and a half yards away. Maximin was still behind the Beautiful Lady but at her right and the same distance away as Melanie herself. That is why he could not see her face. The two shepherds and the Blessed Virgin were still situated in the setting of a wide-open triangle, since Melanie was in front of the Blessed Virgin, but at her left, and Maximin, though behind the Blessed Mother, was somewhat at her right.

The Blessed Virgin accomplished two-thirds of the ascent of the knoll walking in a southeastern course, except for two slight detours. She rose and disappeared in the same general direction. During the Apparition and the Conversation she was turned directly south.

Except while she was seated and rested her head in the open palms of her hands, the Blessed Virgin kept her arms folded and her hands concealed in her large sleeves all the time of the Apparition until her complete disappearance: that is to say, while she descended from the place of the Apparition to the place of the Conversation, all the while that she spoke to the children, when crossing the brook, when ascending the knoll, when she rose and remained in the air a brief moment, and finally when she disappeared.

During the Assumption of the Blessed Virgin, after she had looked up to heaven and lowered her gaze earthward, Melanie's eyes met the sorrowing glance of the Divine Mother. She was no longer weeping but a profound sadness marked her features. So deeply impressed was the little girl by this last look of immense sadness on the countenance of the Beautiful Lady that years later, in 1849, while relating the circumstance, she burst into a flood of tears.

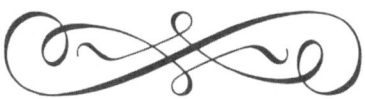

Melanie: *First her head began to disappear – then her arms and then her feet, and that all took place very quickly.*

Maximin: *And then we saw her head no more – then her arms no more and then her feet no more. She seemed to melt away. She vanished suddenly.*

The Blessed Virgin disappeared rapidly; Melanie says "very quickly," and Maximin, "suddenly," meaning very promptly. The various parts of her body vanished in quick succession, first her head and last of all her feet, so rapidly that everything took place in the twinkling of an eye. Her disappearance happened with the same swiftness and in the same order as her appearance. Her first appearing had unrolled before the eyes of the two witnesses with extreme celerity; her disappearance was effected in the same way.

At the moment of her Apparition, the children first saw her head buried in her hands, then her shoulders, then her arms, the rest of her body, and finally her feet. At her disappearance, her head vanished first, then her arms and shoulders, the lower part of her body, and finally her feet. "She seemed to melt away," said the children. During the early days after the Apparition, they sought to convey how it happened in these words: "She melted before our eyes like butter in a frying pan."

Did the Blessed Virgin disappear by vanishing gradually or by entering into a globe of light in such a way that the eyes of the children could no longer follow her? It would seem that at the moment of her disappearance the light around her grew exceedingly strong and bright, thus concealing her person from view.

When she first began to appear, the children could hardly distinguish anything, because of the dazzling light that surrounded her person. When she arose from the stone bench and started to walk along the brook, Melanie remarked that the light became thinner and weaker and remained so all through the Conversation until her Assumption. It is quite likely that at the last moment it became brilliant anew and as dazzling as at the beginning, and thus made her vanish from sight.

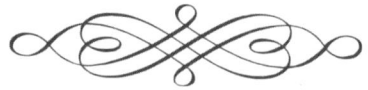

Melanie: *Then Maximin darted his hand out to snatch a little of the bright light but there was nothing there any more.*

Maximin: *I wanted to catch that bright light with my hand as well as the flowers she had at her feet; but there was nothing there any more.*

When Maximin saw that the Beautiful Lady had quite disappeared and that only her feet were visible, he jumped up in the air to reach them with his hand and to seize at least one of the roses that surrounded them. The boy fancied that the light and the roses were something tangible, but as soon as he tried to grasp them everything melted away, the roses and the light.

When the Blessed Virgin disappeared she was still at the level to which she had risen, that is, not quite four feet above the ground. It seemed an easy matter for Maximin to extend his hand and snatch a rose. However, he had to make quite a leap to reach that high; this was necessary since the lad was rather short in stature and he was then standing a little lower than the summit on the steep slope of the knoll. The total distance to cover from the place where he stood to the feet of the Blessed Virgin was not more than two yards. The reason why he jumped so precipitately was not so much the distance involved as the dread of not reaching the roses before they had entirely gone.

Melanie: *And we now saw nothing but a great light in the air. It lasted only an instant and it vanished suddenly at the same height.*

Maximin: *And when she had disappeared we saw a great light at the place where she had risen. It lasted only a brief moment. The bright light was not higher than the very spot where the Lady had been.*

After the disappearance of the Blessed Virgin there remained only a luminous globe like that which filled the ravine the instant she first appeared. Thus the bright light preceded the apparition by a few moments, and it subsisted yet a short while after the disappearance of the Beautiful Lady. The same globe of light did not leave her during the whole period of the Apparition. It vanished immediately after she had disappeared, about four feet above the ground, since it had enveloped her from head to foot.

REFLECTIONS OF THE SHEPHERDS

Melanie: *And I said to Maximin, "It is perhaps a great saint!" And Maximin said to me, "If we had known that it was a great saint we would have told her to take us with her."*

Maximin: *And Melanie said to me, "It must be a great saint!" And I said to her, "If we had known that it was a great saint we would have told her to take us along with her."*

When the shepherds first saw the Blessed Virgin they simply

thought that it was a lady of the vicinity who happened to be passing by. On discovering her seated near his lunch-sack, Maximin believed she wanted to take it from him. When she told them that the arm of her son was "so strong and so heavy" that she could no longer withhold it, they thought it was a mother who had been beaten by her own son and forced to flee into these mountains – or again, a woman whose husband wanted to kill her children.

Later, during the Conversation and until she disappeared, the children formed no other idea about her. They were far too busy looking at her and listening to her to formulate any judgment about her, or about anything else for that matter.

When the Blessed Virgin had completely disappeared, the two children seemed to come out of their trance, and they asked each other who this woman might be. Melanie exclaimed, "It is perhaps a great saint!" She spoke these words after the Beautiful Lady had disappeared but while the light still lingered in the air, since it was these words that determined Maximin to leap promptly and strive to grasp a rose and some of the light around her feet, or rather, at the place from which her feet had just vanished, and where a few of the roses that adorned the soles of her shoes still hung.

What led the girl to believe that this Lady was a great saint was the strange light, brighter than the sun, which enveloped her whole person; also the fact that she rose in the air of her own power and disappeared swiftly and entirely before their very eyes, on this wide-open mountainside and in a sky of clear and stainless blue.

"We would have told her to take us with her," that is, we would have asked her to tell us where she was going – to heaven, no doubt, where the saints abide. For a brief half hour, these children had tasted such bliss in the divine presence of Mary that they could never willingly be separated from her. That is why they had followed her every step, wherever she had turned, and had she chosen to walk about these mountains any farther they would have kept on pursuing her.

While gazing upon her and listening to her words, they forgot all other things, their herds of cattle, their pasture hills, their homes and their people, we might say even their own existence, since during the entire interval they seemed to have no thought of their own. Coming out of a profound rapture, they cried out with regret, "If we had known that it was a great saint, we would have prayed her to take us with her." They did not wish to part from her august presence.

The children did not know who this extraordinary woman might be. They thought she was a saint. She did not tell them her name and they did not ask it of her; how then should they name her? They would give her a name that became her in every respect, one that would serve to describe her most admirably and exactly as she appeared to them – they called her the "Beautiful Lady." The Blessed Virgin herself could hardly have chosen a better name – the "Beautiful Lady," the Lady above all others, the Lady par excellence, the Lady of ravishing beauty. In their childlike way they baptized her the "Beautiful Lady"; and soon after the inhabitants of that region called her Our Lady, and adding the name of the village near which she appeared, they gave her the title, "Our Lady of La Salette."

Thus it did not even enter their minds that this Beautiful Lady might be the Blessed Virgin. They were not the first to claim and to prove that she was indeed the Mother of God. The first person to identify the Beautiful Lady as the Blessed Virgin was Melanie's old mistress, on the very evening of the day of the Apparition; the second was the good old Curé of La Salette; the third was Maximin's master. These are, at least, the first persons who are known to have asserted that it was the Blessed Virgin.

For a long time, even to this very year (1863) the children themselves have never ceased to call her simply the "Beautiful Lady," as they first named her the day they saw her. This has brought forth several objections and has occasioned a sort of scandal on the part of certain persons. These fastidious few were easily unsettled by the fact that the children never used the name of the Blessed Virgin in their recital of the Apparition and always insisted on calling her the Beautiful Lady.

They were all the more flustered when the children, in reply to the question, "Have you ever seen the Blessed Virgin?" warded off the query by saying, "We do not know if it was the Blessed Virgin that we saw, but we have seen a Beautiful Lady who appeared in that manner and spoke such words." To misinterpret the children on this score was proof of the ignorance, the want of reflection, and the bad faith of these persons.

Melanie: *And I said to him, "O that she were still there!" And we looked well to see if we could not see her. And I said, "She will not let herself be seen, that we may not see where she goes."*

"O that she were still there!" that is, in the bright light which had surrounded her and which still lingered a bit before their wondering eyes. The children were made suddenly sad by the disappearance of the Beautiful Lady.

"We looked well," that is, as sharply as their vision permitted as they gazed up in the heavens at the place where the Blessed Virgin had just vanished from sight. They hoped to be able to see her again, perhaps at their side, and wished to follow her wherever she might go. This scene recalls that of the Apostles looking up to heaven at the Ascension of Our Lord (Acts 1:10).

"She will not let herself be seen." These words would have us understand that Melanie believed at first that the Beautiful Lady had hidden herself behind the vanishing light in order that they might not find out which way she was going, lest they might follow her.

Maximin: *After that we were quite content.*

During the Holy Apparition, the two shepherds were, as it were, overflowing with joy and happiness. They could hardly contain the emotions that welled in their hearts. After the disappearance of the Blessed Virgin, these strong and exquisite impressions lingered on a while.

The words of Maximin, "We were quite content," express all that he could say in such circumstances to describe their utter bliss and their inexpressible content. How indeed could the lad describe what he could neither define nor comprehend? This recalls St. Paul's predicament when he tried to reveal what he had seen, heard and felt in the third heaven (2 Corinthians 12:2).

Pra House in hamlet of Les Ablandains near La Salette and interior where the apparition was first retold.

RETURN TO THEIR MASTERS

Melanie: *Then ice went to pick up our little knapsacks. After that we led our cows to our pastures.*

Maximin: *And then we went off to look after our cows.*

After gazing wistfully at the vanishing light and having exchanged their first impressions on the knoll where the Blessed Virgin had just disappeared, the two children came down again to the bed of the ravine to pick up their knapsacks and then went back to tend their cattle on the gentle slope of Mount Gargas. If, as is reported, the girl Melanie did leave her shepherd stick as a marker at the place of the Virgin's Assumption, she must have done so before going down into the ravine, since the two shepherds did not return to the knoll that afternoon.

They went after their cows, made them drink at the brook where they had taken them at noon, and led them off immediately to the southern side of Mount Planeau, in their respective pastures. What hour of day it might have been just then, the children were never quite sure, but most probably it was close to four o'clock.

When they reached their pastures they did not find Pierre Selme mowing hay nearby, as he had done all morning. From the place where he was mowing, Pierre Selme could easily ascertain whether his cattle were safe by simply climbing some four hundred yards toward the summit of Mount Planeau to scan the site of the Apparition. This he must have done that afternoon when Maximin failed to return to him as usual. However, since the boy was with Melanie, who for some months past had kept her flock over these hills, he felt no special anxiety about Maximin's cattle, even though the lad was expected to stay by his side.

Melanie: *And we did not say anything to the other shepherds we saw with their flock a little farther away.*

Melanie here refers to the three little shepherds who had come to drink at the Men's Spring at dinnertime, but had not stayed with them. Had these children not been so far away, Maximin and Melanie might have spoken to them about all they had just seen and heard, but they were quite a distance farther down the mountainside.

Thus from the time of the Apparition until they arrived at the house of their masters, the two shepherds did not meet any one, except perhaps while crossing the hamlet of Dorsières, in which contingency they did not stop to speak with any one about the Apparition.

At any rate, they felt that their masters should be the first to hear about the great vision they had seen, otherwise they might have broken the news to the first person they chanced to meet.

After exchanging their first impressions, the two children resumed their shepherds' games until it was time to lead their cattle back to their masters. True, they had been strongly impressed by what had happened, but their impressions were of a deep calm and sweetness and did not so absorb them as to alter their normal selves. While they were firmly determined to relate all they had seen and heard, as the Lady had charged them to do, they did not otherwise attach very great importance to the matter, and they went on diverting themselves at games as on the previous day. It may seem strange that, having been charged with the greatest mission of our time, they heeded it so little; the fact is that they understood so very little of the wonderful happening.

Melanie: *When I arrived at my master's house I told him about it.*

Maximin: *That evening, when I arrived at my master's house, I felt a bit sad. As they asked me what was the matter with me I told them that I had seen a Lady and I related to them all that this Lady told us.*

After the Apparition, the children took their flock to pasture in the fields where they had kept them before noon. Toward evening, they led their cattle back to their masters' barns, about the same time as on other days, that is, at nightfall. However, it might have been half an hour or three quarters of an hour earlier.

The masters of both Maximin and Melanie dwelt in the hamlet of Ablandins, in the Commune of La Salette, about four miles away from the place of the Apparition. The name of Melanie's master was Baptiste Pra, known as "Caron." He lived with his widowed mother. Maximin's master was Pierre Selme, surnamed "Brouit."

On September 19, Pierre Selme spent most of the day cutting hay with a scythe, on the southern slope of Mount Planeau, some four hundred yards from the place of the Apparition. The children watched their flocks on the northern side of the same mountain. Pierre Selme returned home at the Ablandins before the two shepherds led their cattle back to their allotted pastures.

"I felt a bit sad." The word "sad" in Maximin's vocabulary did not signify that he felt either worried or lonely or afflicted. It meant, rather, that contrary to his usual habit he appeared more serious and pensive than was his wont on other days. Upon arriving at the Ablandins, the lad found it necessary to justify himself to his master, who reproached him for failing to return to him in the afternoon at the usual time.

In the meantime, the girl Melanie was busy milking her cows, and she had determined not to say a word about the event until her chores were done. The mission which she had received seemed less important at the moment than the milking of her cows. She manifested no greater eagerness in acquitting herself of Our Lady's injunction because she really understood nothing as yet of the celestial Apparition.

Maximin was a rather frequent visitor at the house of Mr. Pra, Melanie's master, who lived next door. During the year preceding the Apparition, the boy called from time to time to see his sister, who was a servant maid in the Pra household. Thus as soon as he had related the event of the Apparition to his own master, Mr. Selme, he went over to Pra's house and rehearsed it again before the girl Melanie was through milking her cows. The girl's mistress later reproved her for not having reported sooner what they had seen and heard on the mountain.

How the News Spread

Here is the sequence of events which marked the transmission of the great news on the day of the Apparition. First, Maximin spoke of it to his master when the latter rebuked him for not returning to him in his field that afternoon. Amazed at what the shepherd told him, Pierre Selme asked the boy if Melanie also had seen and heard this Beautiful Lady. Upon Maximin's affirmative reply, Selme went with him immediately to Pra's house, where the boy repeated his recital.

After that, Maximin, Mr. Selme, Mr. Pra and the latter's mother went out to the stable where Melanie was still busy milking her cows, for she had not yet gone into the house. They asked her whether Maximin told the truth, and she answered, "Yes, it is so," but said no more. Her mistress, Mr. Pra's elderly mother, bade her leave her cows and go into the house, where she related to them, as Maximin had already done, all that the Beautiful Lady had told them. The children's masters were satisfied that the two reports were identical in content. They at once spread the word throughout the village, and in no time everyone had heard about it.

Thus, on that very evening, these two frail-looking children were transformed into young apostles of the Apparition. A few hours after the event, they began to fulfill the great mission which the Beautiful Lady confided to them in these words: "Well, my children, you will make this known to all my people."

Without addition or subtraction, they reported most faithfully what they had heard and seen. At first, people scoffed at them and made fun of their report, but soon laughter gave way to a holy fear, a fear inspired by the spoken threats of the Beautiful Lady, and ultimately belief in the children's message prevailed.

On that first day, only Melanie's old mistress accepted as indubitable the account of the Apparition, and she alone took really to heart the words of the Blessed Virgin. Many others also believed but not so completely, because their hearts were not as simple and upright as was this good soul's.

On the following day, quite a few took the report more seriously, among whom was Melanie's master, Baptiste Pra. This man had planned to chop wood on that Sunday, but he was wholesomely frightened by the ominous reproofs of the Beautiful Lady, and abstained from doing so. From that day on he never allowed his farmhands to do any servile work on Sundays and holy days.

All those who heard the children's recital could not but be impressed thereat, and only a small minority of heedless folk scoffed at it and refused to believe what they had heard. On the night of September 19, 1846 and for several weeks thereafter, the children delivered the account of the Apparition with animated tone and an air of conviction far surpassing the ordinary.

They presented a strange contrast to their usual uncouth appearance and ignorance, especially the shy girl Melanie, who seldom showed the least enthusiasm for anything. Little did they resemble the uninteresting shepherds they had been on the morning of that same day. This change struck their listeners with amazement and brought about ready signs of conviction in them, or at least a disposition to believe after further reflection and investigation.

On that day, and even after, the children were content to relate, word for word, the discourse of the Beautiful Lady, giving but few if any details on the Apparition itself. As soon as they were through reciting the words of the Blessed Virgin, they kept silence. One might have thought that this was absolutely all they knew. Nevertheless, they always answered promptly and clearly all the questions put to them.

Thus people began to ply them with a thousand various questions, which from the very first day served to make known many interesting details on the event of the Apparition, details which, when collected, sifted and harmonized into a composite whole, completed the moral teaching contained in the discourse of the Beautiful Lady.

Melanie: *He told me that I must go and tell it to the Curé of La Salette. I told Maximin so and we went on Sunday morning. The Curé wrote it down and told it at Mass.*

Maximin: *My master told me to go and tell it to the Curé of La Salette. The next day, Sunday, Melanie came to get me to go to the Curé's house at La Salette and I went with her. We told it to him and he told us to go and tell it to the Curé here at Corps.*

The two persons who first told the children to go and relate the Apparition to the Curé of La Salette were Melanie's mistress and Baptiste Pra, the son of this elderly widow. Many other persons of the hamlet of Ablandins also urged the children to take this action. The first to send the shepherds to the Curé of the parish, however, were their own masters. On Sunday morning, Sept. 20, 1846, Melanie called at the house where Maximin lived to take him with her to the rectory as their masters had recommended them to do the previous night. When they arrived at the rectory, the housekeeper would not permit them to speak to the Curé, who was probably busy preparing his Sunday announcements. She naturally believed that they had nothing very important to tell and that she could very well take care of their message herself.

Upon her request, the children began to relate the story of the Apparition. Somehow, the Curé heard part of the conversation from his study, and when they were done with the recital he came to them in the kitchen and made them repeat what they had just related to the housekeeper. Upon hearing their moving account, he broke into tears and declared that doubtless they had seen the Blessed Virgin. Immediately the good Curé jotted down a few notes from their narrative, and an hour or two later he spoke about it in his sermon to the faithful.

This venerable Curé was Father Jacques Perrin, a very plain and pious priest of God, then aged sixty-three. At the time of the Apparition, his health was not of the best and he had already been assigned to a post situated in a milder clime than that of the mountainous region of La Salette, where he had been stationed for the past fourteen years. He left the parish of La Salette on November 10, 1846.

His successor, a young priest of the same name, Father Michel Perrin, arrived in his new parish on September 26 that same year. He spent twelve days with his worthy predecessor. Though young and energetic, the new Curé of La Salette was soon unable to cope with his growing task, because of the large concourse of pilgrims to the Holy Mountain. For this reason, Monsignor de Bruillard, Bishop of Grenoble, sent him, as assistant, his own brother, Abbé Louis Perrin, Chaplain of the General Hospital of Grenoble. They were good and holy priests.

Melanie: *After that Maximin returned to Corps.*

Maximin: *Melanie stayed and I returned with my master to my father's house.*

After they told their narrative to the Curé of La Salette, the two children separated. Melanie returned to stay at her master's house until the middle of November of that year, and Maximin left immediately with his master, who took him back to his father at Corps. From that day on, except for a few occasions when they accompanied pilgrims to the Holy Mountain, Melanie and Maximin did not see each other nor speak to each other until Christmas of that year. Each told the story of the Apparition separately.

Upon his return to Corps, Maximin wanted to relate to his Curé what had happened on the mountain, but the latter, not deeming it anything of importance, and being rather busy that day, told the lad to return on the morrow. It was then on Monday, Sept. 21, that Father Mélin, Curé of Corps, first heard the recital of the marvelous Apparition.

MAXIMIN 1846

MELANIE 1846

THE WITNESSES OF THE APPARITION

MAXIMIN
PAPAL ZOUAVE

MELANIE
AT PALERMO 1896

PART FOUR – THE WOMAN BEAUTIFUL

THE VISION DESCRIBED

Maximin: *She was all white.*

Maximin does not mean that the whole attire of the Blessed Virgin was white since part of her raiment was of various colors. He simply means that the person of the Beautiful Lady appeared all white, particularly from the viewpoint then implied. "We crossed the brook," says the boy, "we were following her; she was all white," Mary's raiment, viewed from Maximin's position when walking in her footsteps, was entirely white in appearance, except for the golden chainwork and the garlands of roses which were wound over her shoulders.

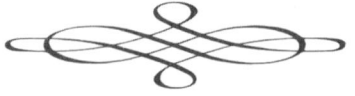

Melanie: *She was slender and tall, taller than an ordinary woman, taller than any woman I had ever seen.*

Maximin: *She was very tall, taller than other women.*

The Blessed Virgin appeared to be of rather high stature. The children say she was very tall, taller than any women they had ever seen. They strove thus to describe her exactly as she appeared to them. In order to understand correctly just what they meant, we must first recall that the children themselves were rather small for their age. Then also we must remember that during the Apparition the Blessed Virgin stood three or four inches above the ground. Finally, her headdress and her diadem reached up about four or five inches above her head. Thus we conclude that, in reality, the Blessed Virgin was no taller than most women. To the children's eyes, measuring from the ground over which she stood to the summit of her diadem, she appeared to exceed the average height.

"She was slender," says Melanie. The fact that her feet did not rest upon the ground and that she wore a rather high headdress helped to create this impression of slimness. The light under her feet as well as over her diadem seemed to be part of her body, from which it emanated. This also enhanced her slenderness of form. The word "slender" in the girl's vocabulary contrasted with the word "ample," but did not imply that the Blessed Virgin seemed gaunt or thin. The fact also that her garments lay lightsomely on her body, without ampler filling than dignity and decency required, added no little to the impression of slimness.

The august person of Mary was modeled after the ideal archetype of Womanhood, not to be compared with other women. Nothing on earth can give us a true conception of the beauty which the children contemplated in the person of our Blessed Mother.

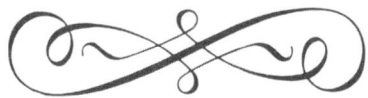

Melanie: *I could not very well consider her person nor look at her long, because she dazzled me. Every now and then we rubbed our eyes and then looked on anew.*

Maximin: *When I looked at her she dazzled me so that I could not keep looking on.*

The children found it quite difficult to gaze steadily upon the Blessed Virgin, because the light which emanated from her person, and particularly from her countenance, scintillated more vividly than the light of the sun. Every now and then they were obliged to rub their eyes in order to clarify their vision. This they did several times; first, when she began to appear in the midst of a great light, and then again and again, during the conversation when their gaze centered chiefly upon the features of the Beautiful Lady.

The strange light which surrounded the Blessed Virgin did not, however, injure their eyes, nor did it give forth heat. The children suffered no more than a passing inconvenience from the dazzling effect of the light. Their greatest annoyance came from striving to contemplate too closely the countenance of the Blessed Virgin. Maximin failed entirely to distinguished her features, and Melanie was only slightly more successful. Both of them experienced a blurring and clouding of their sight. A certain mist seemed to fill their eyes, and by rubbing them intermittently with their hands they endeavored to clear them from this filmy obstruction, so as to obtain a clearer view of the Beautiful Lady.

HER COUNTENANCE

Melanie: *However, I observed that she had a very lovely face. It was very pale, but shapely, not quite small, somewhat oval and very beautiful. Her eyebrows were dark and not too heavy. Her countenance was sad.*

Maximin: *I was not able to see her face. We could hardly look at it; it dazzled us so.*

The patois word *blantzinella (whitish),* which Melanie used to indicate the white complexion of Our Lady's visage, signifies literally neither white nor livid, but a tint of pallor. It designates that pallid hue which marks the features of persons who are on the verge of sickness, children especially, or of persons convalescing from a long illness; also of persons who are overwhelmed by an immense sadness or seized with consuming sorrow.

Maximin was not at all able to view the features of the Blessed Virgin, despite the great efforts he made to see them. He saw all of her person from her feet up to her chin, and from the middle of her forehead to her diadem, but not her face. Upon her celestial visage shone a very bright and vivid light, which dazzled him so that he could discern neither shape, nor color, nor facial traits.

He did perceive, as it were a human countenance, but far too indistinctly to call this "seeing" in the real sense of the word. He was right, therefore, in saying that he did not see the face of the Beautiful Lady. What a lesson of modesty the Queen of Virgins gave us on that occasion!

Even though Melanie could not gaze steadily and clearly at the face of the Divine Mother, she was able nevertheless to remark that it was extremely beautiful. All this beauty, which neither human language nor painter's brush can describe, she rendered in these plain yet expressive words: "She had a very lovely face." She stressed this twice in her recital.

The countenance of Our Lady of La Salette was oval-shaped and white. It was not a sheer marble whiteness, but rather a soft gleaming pallor. Though sadness might have diminished the brightness of her features, it seemed not to have tarnished their splendor. Sorrow did not dull the radiance of her countenance.

Her face seemed molded after the archetype of the Woman Beautiful. Nothing in creation can quite convey the faintest idea of its regularity and harmony of shape and complexion. If Melanie's imperfect view of this exquisite masterpiece of feminine perfection revealed but a token of its matchless beauty, only the saints and the angels in heaven can come nearer to the reality.

While the whole person of the Blessed Virgin radiated light, her face shone with a brightness all its own. In the midst of the great globe of light it seemed like the sun amid all creation, with this difference only, that in comparison with it the noonday sun itself appeared dull and, as it were, a mere shadow.

We need not wonder that the boy Maximin was unable to see the face of the Beautiful Lady; the marvel is that Melanie was able to glimpse it momentarily, despite its blinding brilliance. It was a rare privilege for Melanie to scan even so briefly the peerless face of Mary, upon which angels and saints alone may gaze with ease in the august courts of Heaven. Ever since that signal privilege was granted to Melanie, everything earthly, the splendor of the sun itself, became unattractive and even unsightly to her eyes.

The visage of the Beautiful Lady was stamped with profound sadness, but this sadness in no way dimmed or marred the celestial beauty of her features. Melanie described this sadness as a veil settling upon her countenance without, however, obscuring its splendor. It is difficult to conceive such perfect blending of deep sorrow and radiant beauty, yet the two coexisted with striking distinctness.

It was impossible for Melanie to discern the color of the eyes of the Blessed Virgin; first, because she could not fix her gaze upon them clearly enough; second, because the Blessed Virgin kept them lowered; and third, because they were dimmed with tears.

In Melanie's words, the face of the Beautiful Lady was "not quite small and somewhat oval," and her eyebrows were "dark and not too heavy." By this she means that every feature of her countenance was admirably regular and fitted into a harmonious design of perfect symmetry. Here indeed was the Woman Perfect, fresh as it were from the hands of the Creator, the Woman par excellence, the *Mother of God.*

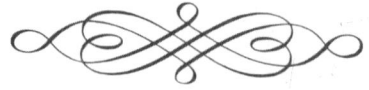

Melanie: *I looked at her face two or three times. I noticed that when she spoke to us her eyes were lowered and she gazed downward.*

During the Conversation, which lasted about half an hour, Melanie looked upon the face of the Blessed Virgin two or three times only. Most of the time she kept looking at the feet of the Beautiful Lady.

That is why, whenever she was asked to describe the manner of dress of the Divine Mother, she always began her delineation by telling of the shoes she wore.

All through the Conversation the Blessed Virgin kept her eyes modestly lowered. She did not gaze at the children fixedly. Her eyes seemed rather to hover benevolently over them. Because of the short stature of the children and of their close proximity, she had to incline her head in order to hold them both in the same comprehensive look.

While speaking to the two shepherds, the attitude of the Beautiful Lady was all modesty and simplicity. She breathed such sweetness and affability that the children felt quite at ease in her benign presence and as free as if she had been their own mother. Yet her bearing was so stately, so dignified and majestic, that she commanded their most profound respect.

Melanie: *She stood straight. Her arms were folded and her head was slightly inclined.*

Maximin: *She stood erect and her head leaned gently forward.*

The Blessed Virgin stood erect all the while that she spoke to the children. She kept her arms folded, right over left, upon her breast. Her head leaned slightly forward as she gazed on them both without fixedly looking them in the face. The fact that she stood three or four inches above the ground, and that the children were rather short in stature and quite close to her, obliged her to bend her head toward them while addressing them. She did not look at them straight in the face or in the eye; her gaze simply embraced them both. She remained in that position throughout the discourse, and only when delivering to each a secret or when questioning them separately did she turn slightly to address the one or the other.

Melanie: *She simply gazed upon us. Her eyes were extremely pleasant. She looked on us with great kindliness and so sweetly that she drew us to herself in spite of ourselves.*

The person of the Blessed Virgin, and her tender look in particular, held the children, as it were, under a spell. So strong was this attraction that, toward the end of the Apparition, they could hardly bear to be separated from her. Maximin experienced this feeling even though he had hardly glimpsed her face. Her gaze held such power and sweetness that, as Melanie expressed it, she drew them to her in spite of themselves. The children felt constrained to love her and to remain close to her.

Just before disappearing, while she was still raised in the air, the Blessed Virgin cast one last look upon Melanie, who stood facing her. At that particular moment the shepherd girl observed the deep sadness which stamped her features. In that last glance there was such keen sorrow blended with charming sweetness that Melanie felt as if her heart were pierced with a dart.

HER VOICE

Melanie: *Her voice sounded like music.*

Maximin: *Her voice was sweet as music. It seemed as if we ate her words.*

The voice of the Blessed Virgin was extremely sweet and melodious. It sounded to the children's ears like a rich, harmonious concert of the most delightful musical instruments, and far sweeter, since it was sheer celestial music.

The two children could never explain exactly in what manner they heard the heavenly words of the Beautiful Lady; whether they first apprehended them through the sense of hearing and then received them in their hearts, or whether they perceived them solely and directly through their heart. They could not tell through what channel the words reached their inmost soul. It seemed as if each word penetrated their very bosom instantly, having no need to travel through the ordinary medium of hearing.

The words uttered by the Blessed Virgin were not merely harmonious sounds but rather an exquisitely delectable and comforting substance which invaded their heart more like a celestial aliment, which they promptly absorbed. In their childlike simplicity, they declared that her words were rather edible than audible. "It seemed as if we ate her words." Truly, her voice flowed into their ears and distilled into their hearts.

Melanie: *When she spoke to us we thought of nothing else. We just stood there.*

Maximin: *While she spoke to us we thought of nothing else. We said not a word. We remained standing and simply listened.*

While the Blessed Virgin spoke, the two children stood facing her without uttering a word. They were so strongly impressed and so completely absorbed by what they saw and heard that they seemed to be rapt in a sort of ecstasy, having quite lost their self-consciousness. The Beautiful Lady was the all-absorbing interest of the moment. They stood silent and attentive.

Until the Beautiful Lady had first addressed them with these words, "Come near, my children, be not afraid," diverse thoughts and various surmises had entered their minds. Again, after she had disappeared, they recovered normal consciousness and began to entertain certain conjectures regarding this Lady. During her discourse and Conversation they surrendered to her ravishing spell and lapsed into a form of profound rapture.

This temporary exaltation did not, however, deprive them of their full awareness regarding what transpired in their presence. All their senses were keenly responsive to the reality about them. Their eyes and ears and minds and hearts functioned with unerring vividness, and bore sure testimony of all that was taking place before them. If anything, they perceived with even greater intensity the detailed and impressive miracle which unfurled before their wondering eyes.

Melanie: *The sun was shining, yet she cast no shadow. When we came down the knoll and when we moved about at a distance from her we cast our own shadows, but when we stood near her, there wasn't any shadow.*

Maximin: *The sun was shining brightly.*

On the day and at the moment of the Apparition, the skies were exceptionally clear and the sun shone in all its noonday splendor. Such warm and ideal weather was quite unusual on these mountain heights in the early autumn season. In fact, the day after the Apparition there was a sudden drop in temperature, and it rained.

The light which surrounded the Blessed Virgin was so brilliant that it robbed the sun of its splendor. To the children who stood near the Beautiful Lady, all nature appeared somewhat as it does to a person who, in the middle of the night, happens to stand by a huge bonfire, which casts a strong light about while darkness hovers over all else.

When the two shepherds stood near the Beautiful Lady, they observed that no shadow was projected either by her body or by their own. They remarked this strange phenomenon from the very beginning. After the Apparition, they noticed that their bodies did cast a shadow. This observation on the part of the children is very important. It invincibly proves that the mysterious person who appeared to them was not of this earth. It is well known that the lightest and the frailest object, be it even a burning flame, will in the full glow of the sun, project some shadow. So bright and lightsome was the body of the Blessed Virgin that it failed to cast a shadow of its own, and, what is still more remarkable, it caused the shadows of the shepherds themselves to vanish. It even eclipsed the sun into a dull and somber disk.

Her Raiment

Melanie: *She wore white shoes with a garland of roses around the sole. There were roses of all colors. On each shoe lay a square buckle of bright gold. There were also pearls on her shoes.*

Maximin: *Her shoes were white and there were roses around them. Over the arch of each foot lay a golden buckle.*

The shoes worn by the Beautiful Lady were sparkling white and bestrewn with gems, as was her full, white robe. Encircling the soles were garlands of tiny roses, much smaller than those which bordered her crown and kerchief. These roses were of various colors, chiefly white, red, blue, pink and even other colors which natural roses are not known to display.

In shape and style the shoes of the Beautiful Lady resembled the low shoes worn by the ordinary women of that part of France. The buckles on top of the shoes were the color of bright gold. They were rather narrow in shape than perfectly square, and lay from the top of the arch to the tip of the shoe.

When describing the costume or raiment of the Beautiful Lady, the children, especially on the first days following the Apparition, began by telling of her footwear, and continued their description of her person in the ascending order, concluding with her crown and headgear. This may have been largely due to the fact that all through the apparition they were unable to view the Blessed Virgin's face with ease, and they found it more convenient to gaze almost constantly at her feet. To all intent, we can note here a particular design of the Mother of God, giving to the world, in the persons of the two little shepherds, a striking lesson of Christian modesty.

Melanie: *While she spoke to us, I considered only her shoes, and I gave no heed to the stockings she wore. It was only when I ascended the knoll that I glimpsed at these. They were a ruddy gold.*

During the Conversation, Melanie did not observe the stockings of the Beautiful Lady because her long robe reached down to her very shoes, and covered part of them. However, when following in the footsteps of the Blessed Virgin as she ascended the steep hillock, the girl did accidentally, if not by a stealthy glance, manage to glimpse very rapidly this item of her apparel. The boy, Maximin, less observant than his companion, never mentioned this detail, though he kept much closer to the Beautiful Lady and watched her every step. Here again we learn another lesson of modesty taught to men by the Queen of Heaven.

Except for this minor item of Our Lady's costume, both Maximin and Melanie, from the very first days, gave an identical description of her person. However, in this respect the little girl was more closely questioned, since she was presumed to be more observant than the boy. Nevertheless, it would be false to hold that Maximin did not clearly observe the diverse parts of the Beautiful Lady's apparel.

Melanie declared that the stockings of the Beautiful Lady were a brilliant gold, as were also her apron and her kerchief. Her dress and her shoes, though likewise of plain material, glittered still more with gems and bright spangles.

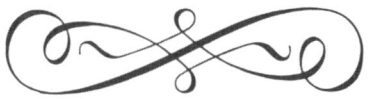

Melanie: *She wore a white dress entirely covered with bright gems. The sleeves were large. She did not show her hands.*

Maximin: *She wore a white dress. There were pearls strewn all over it. The sleeves were long and broad. We did not see her hands. She kept them always folded one over the other or in her sleeves.*

The robe worn by Our Lady of La Salette was entirely white, of plain cloth, yet bestrewn with glittering pearls or spangles of light. The material of Our Lady's dress seemed coarse, rather than fine, in texture. The style of the dress was modest and austere in design, neither too ample nor too close fitting. The robe draped her body without accentuating its contour, and it reached straight down to her feet. It covered her throat and neck and extended to the lower part of her headdress.

The sleeves of her dress were long and broad, not unlike the sleeves of a Sister's habit. Said the children: "Her sleeves were old-style," meaning that they were long and straight, extending a few inches beyond the tips of her fingers and covering her forearms evenly. They concealed her hands, which lay folded, right over left, upon her breast, each hand within its own sleeve.

Only when the Beautiful Lady was first seen weeping and covering her face with her hands was Melanie able to observe that her hands were extremely white. At that moment also the girl noticed the narrow under-sleeves that covered her forearm up to her wrist.

Melanie: *Her apron was the color of brilliant gold. It extended as far down as the hem of her dress over her feet.*

Maximin: *Her apron was the color of gold.*

While the apron worn by the Beautiful Lady seemed brilliant as gold, it appeared to be of plain cloth and texture, devoid of pearls or flowers or any artistic design. This broad apron hung at the cincture and covered the front of her dress down to almost half an inch from the extreme hem of her garment. It was not the sort of apron worn for mere display; if anything, it resembled the housewife's apron, worn for domestic work, like that of country women and servant maids.

The color of the apron was described by the children as "yellow." In their plain language this designated a gold tone of color, sparkling pure and unalloyed, like the rays of the sun or the brightest ingot. Never could they discover in nature anything that could adequately suggest the color they thus attempted to describe.

The same word is used to indicate the color of the buckles on her shoes, the chainwork of gold braid on the border of her kerchief, the small chain around her neck, and the crucifix that hung therefrom. The other items of her apparel were snow-white, namely, her shoes, her robe, her kerchief, and her headgear. Thus white and gold formed the prevailing color scheme of her raiment. Only the many-colored roses which encircled her feet, her breast, and her head gave any variety to the pattern.

Rose Garlands

Melanie: *The kerchief she wore was white as was her dress; but there were no pearls upon it. It reached down well over her arms and it was bordered with roses of all sorts of colors. The corner folds of the kerchief crossed in front at her cincture and were knotted together in the back.*

Maximin: *She wore a white kerchief with roses on it that were tied together like a garland. There were large roses and small roses.*

The Beautiful Lady wore a kerchief, or cape, of the same color and cloth as the robe, but plainer in this respect, that it did not gleam with resplendent gems of jeweled light. Nevertheless, the border of the kerchief was trimmed with roses and a sort of thin, golden braid which the children called the "large chain." The kerchief reached down well over her arms, says Melanie; not that it lay over her wrist or her forearm, since it came down only as far as the elbows.

This kerchief was not a mere neck scarf, but rather a sort of cape or shawl such as are worn by the women of that region of France, or of any other country, for that matter. It covered the shoulders and the breast of the Beautiful Lady, but it did not quite cover that part of her robe which extended to her head-dress and covered her throat and neck. The corner folds of the ker-chief crossed in front, covering her breast entirely, the two ends being knotted at the back of the waist. This overlapping kerchief added a graceful touch of modesty to the costume of the celestial Visitor.

The garland of many-colored roses which adorned the border of her kerchief was not mere embroidery or fringe; it lay upon the cloth at about a finger's width from the hem. According to Maxi-min's recital, these roses were not all of equal dimension. The ros-es set upon the corner folds of the kerchief were much smaller than those which lay over her breast and shoulders. They diminished in size gradually as they reached the corner ends of the folded ker-chief.

Beside the garland of roses, along the border of the kerchief, there lay a flat band of gold braid, which, for want of a more adequate expression, the children called "the large chain," to distinguish it no doubt from the smaller chain around her neck, which held a golden crucifix. It may also be noted that Melanie saw rays of light issuing from the roses on her kerchief, as was also the case with the roses at her feet and on her head.

Our Lady of La Salette wore a kerchief that appears quite different from the sort of apparel sometimes worn by worldly women. It is clear from the description made of her modest kerchief that it cannot be classed with such neck scarves as are worn rather as an excuse for womanly dress; nor is it such extravagant finery as the overly wrought mantillas of rich ladies.

Melanie: *Along the garland of roses that bordered her kerchief there lay, on the inner side, toward the shoulder, a long chain about three fingers wide. It was the color of gold.*

Maximin: *She also wore a chain some three fingers wide. It was gold-colored and lay flat alongside the garland of roses.*

A finger's breadth above the garland of roses on her kerchief lay a large chain, or rather a band of gold braid resembling a chain. The braid was some three fingers wide and consisted of flat rectangular pieces of gold texture, like the closely set but unconnected links of a large chain. Unable to find words to describe this bright band of material, the children called it a large chain, but when asked to compare it with some large chains of the kind worn by women of that region of the country they rather invariably chose to compare it with the gold-braid design found on sacerdotal vestments, for instance, the border of a chasuble. The parts of the chainlike ornament were thin pieces of woven texture laid side by side without interlacing. Together with the garland of roses, this gold braid bordered all the kerchief, front and back, passed underneath the crucifix on her breast, and disappeared under her folded arms.

Her Chain and Crucifix

Melanie: *She also wore a small golden chain hung around her neck. It held a cross with the figure of Christ. This cross extended from the middle of her breast down to her folded arms. Upon the cross, at each extremity, there were pliers on the right and a hammer on the left. These were golden-colored and seemed to hold on to nothing.*

Maximin: *She wore a small chain that held a cross. This cross hung from her neck down to her folded arms. There were pliers and a hammer upon the arms of the cross.*

This small chain, apparently of the same material as the large one, was about one-third of an inch in width. It held a cross suspended on the breast of the Blessed Virgin. This cross was seven or eight inches in length. It was golden and extremely brilliant. The foot of the cross rested an inch or two beneath the sleeves of her folded arms.

The figure of Christ was brilliant gold, much brighter even than the cross itself. This cross and the large chain-work around her kerchief were among the brightest objects on her person, but the figure of Christ far surpassed these in light and beauty. No other article of her apparel was quite as luminous and resplendent.

The hammer and pliers were not fixed on the arms of the cross. They were set at each extremity about an inch away from the crossbeam. Persons who have seen a crucifix of Our Lady of La Salette can easily understand this by imagining that the hammer and pliers stand a slight distance from the cross. The pliers were half open. The handle of the hammer and those of the pliers extended below the crossbeam and the head of these instruments stood out above it.

This cross with the figure of Christ and the hammer and pliers shone like bright gold, but the cross was brighter than the hammer and pliers, and the figure of Christ was still more luminous than the cross. The children have indicated with a gesture the exact position of this cross on the breast of the Beautiful Lady. It hung below the neck on the middle of her breast and extended beneath the folds of her sleeves.

Melanie: *Her headdress rose quite high over her head, broad in the back and slightly bent forward at the top. The rim came down to the middle of her forehead above her eyes, over her temples and along the outline of her face. I did not notice any lace and I do not know of what material it was made. It was all white. It was not attached under her chin.*

Maximin: *She wore a head-covering broad and high. Its rim came down almost to her eyes.*

The Beautiful Lady wore a high headdress much in the style of a peasant bonnet or cap, somewhat conical in shape but rounded and turned forward at the top. Together with the luminous rays which issued therefrom and formed one and the same ornamental headpiece with it, this covering reached the height of six or seven inches above her head.

The rim of this bonnet-like headdress was not lined with lace but with a sort of piping cloth, finely plaited. It seemed quite a huge headgear to the children, and different from the elegant and frail excuses for hats of modern feminine creation. However it appeared very becoming and in no way detracted from the ravishing beauty of the Queen of Heaven and Earth.

This headdress was entirely white. It was not embroidered. There was no ribbon to attach it under the chin. The children could not say of what sort of cloth it seemed to be made. They did not remark any kind of lace around it. The rim was plain cloth plaited like light muslin. It came down quite low on her forehead, covering her hair and her ears entirely and joining the scarf-like part of her dress around her neck. It ran down her temples and framed her features with neat and graceful outline.

The crown which adorned her headdress was distinct from it yet it greatly enhanced its design. This crown was set horizontally on her forehead and circled above her ears. The boy Maximin could distinctly perceive the head of the Blessed Virgin from the middle of her forehead to the summit of her headdress, but not the underlying zone of her features.

In modesty and simplicity of style. Our Lady's headdress offered a condemnation of the millinery extravagance in vogue among the women of the world. Nevertheless, enhanced with a rich and brilliant crown, this plain covering rose like a royal diadem or a tiara adorning the Queen of Angels and of her people.

Her Royal Crown

Melanie: *Around her head she wore a very beautiful crown of roses of all colors like those on her kerchief, and there were other very brilliant things. This crown encircled her headdress without touching it.*

Maximin: *She wore a crown made all around of very lovely roses and other things. The crown did not touch her headdress; it was set there as though it rested on air.*

The crown which encircled the head of the Blessed Virgin was strung with roses of all colors, that is to say, not only of colors such as we commonly find in natural roses, but of all varied tints found elsewhere in nature. The roses of the crown were rather large as were also those on her kerchief. They were about half the size of natural roses. Those of the crown and kerchief were mostly all of this dimension, but those around her feet were all small.

All the roses on her person, whether on her crown or on her kerchief or on her shoes, were multicolored roses. The two little shepherds christened them "roses" because these brilliant creations assumed the form of roses, yet nowhere in the fair realm of nature did the children ever see anything apt to suggest an idea that might approach the reality of their vision.

From her crown of roses there sprung tiny flowers of gold and silver in varied patterns. They seemed to soar above the base of the garland of roses and raise the height of the coronet by some five or six inches. Rays of light flashed from the heart of these flowers. Clusters of sparks burst between each sheaf of stems and flowers. It was a sheer fabric of rich, sparkling and dazzling elements.

This royal crown did not rest upon her headdress. It seemed to lean on air. It apparently was held in place by nothing. It was slightly larger in perimeter than the head which it encircled. It lay horizontally on the middle of her forehead, grazed her ears, and came down beyond her temples. It was not a mere coronet; it was a splendid diadem.

The stems and flowers which rose from its base spread out wider at the summit, reaching the height of six or seven inches above her forehead. The out-branching rays of light diminishing in height toward the back of her head. This masterpiece of divine artistry formed a superb tiara somewhat similar to those worn by the kings and queens among the Jews of old.

The raiment of Our Lady of La Salette seemed to be made of extremely plain, simple, ordinary, almost coarse material. Yet upon her dress and her shoes were pearls and gemlike spangles. These radiant gems issued like dots of light from the incandescent luminosity of her person.

Each article of her apparel was either entirely white or entirely gold-colored, since these were the dominant colors adopted as the color scheme of her costume. Thus the greater part of her vesture was white, namely, her shoes, her dress, her kerchief, and her headdress. Golden were the buckles on her shoes, her stockings, her apron, the chain-work braid on her kerchief, and her small chain and her crucifix.

Here is the full list of her apparel: white low shoes strewn with pearls, surrounded with garlands of small roses of various colors and surmounted with golden buckles; golden-hued stockings; the dress entirely white and covered with spangles; long, broad sleeves and smaller undersleeves reaching to her wrists; a gold-colored apron, very long and broad; a white kerchief bordered with a garland of multicolored roses and gold braid; a small golden chain holding a gold crucifix with pliers and hammer; a white headdress girded with a crown of roses and graced with a royal diadem of luminous flowers and sparkling gems.

In regard to style and material, the costume of the Blessed Virgin was very plain, modest, decent and of austere appearance, yet not lacking in grace and majesty. Her only finery consisted of rose garlands, buckles and lacework, and a bejeweled diadem. The astounding simplicity of her dress was set off by the resplendent light which seemed to issue from her luminous body and permeate her garment. The plain articles of her vesture possessed no glory of their own; intimating that the raiment does not adorn the person so well as the person enhances the raiment. Christian womanhood may learn many a striking lesson in the costume of Our Lady of La Salette.

Last Reflections

Melanie: *And we said that it was all very lovely. After she had dis-appeared, Maximin said to me, "O how beautiful she was!" What he found prettiest of all was her cross, and I, both her neckerchief and her cross. And we both said that what we thought was alto-gether finest of all was the chain and the cross.*

Maximin: *And we talked about everything we had seen.*

During the Apparition, the children spoke not a word to each other, but as soon as the Blessed Virgin had disappeared they began to exchange their impressions about all they had found bright and beautiful in the person of the Beautiful Lady. They did not rehearse what she had said either to both of them together or to each in particular. The reason for their mutual reticence lay in the fact that they had both heard her full Discourse, and regarding what she had told each in particular, that is, their secret, she had forbidden them to reveal it to anyone, including themselves respectively.

All in all, they said very little to each other concerning the Apparition; they simply communicated to each other their most striking impressions of the Beautiful Lady. After that they conversed on other things and amused themselves at shepherds' games as they might have done any other day.

Most striking among the several items of her apparel were the large chainwork of golden lace around her kerchief and the crucifix on her breast. Maximin considered the crucifix of the Blessed Virgin and the figure of Christ in particular as by far the most marvelous object on her person. Melanie was also strongly impressed by her kerchief, not for its own value, since it was plain and devoid of spangles, but uniquely because of the large chainwork of golden lace which bordered it and shone with extreme brilliancy.

The two children agreed in their judgment regarding the loveliest and brightest object – the crucifix on her breast. True, the diadem on her head must have seemed equally beautiful, perhaps even finer and richer, but the Blessed Virgin evidently willed that the chain and the cross should appear more ravishing to their eyes than any other item of her apparel. To all Christians, indeed, the Cross of the Crucified Lord is the loveliest and most precious treasure in the world.

Prayer to Our Lady of La Salette

To the Queen of Heaven and Earth, the August Mary, our tender and well-beloved Mother, who deigned to show herself on the Holy Mountain of La Salette in order to communicate her celestial warnings to her people, through the means of two little shepherds, two poor and ignorant children, on whose lips she deposited an all-heavenly wisdom, be love, honor, glory, gratitude, praise and benediction, on earth as in Heaven, here and throughout the whole world; today, tomorrow and forever, in time and in eternity. May the Sovereignty of Our Lady of La Salette soon extend unto the far-limits of the earth. Amen.

Part Five - As They Saw Her

As She Chose Them

The privileged witnesses of Our Lady's Appearance at La Salette had little to recommend them from human standards alone, yet they caught the fancy of Mary as best suited to carry out her design. They were gifted with remarkable powers of observation. Alert as never before, nothing escaped their keen eyes and ears. Sights and sounds of unearthly charm absorbed their faculties in the contemplation of the Beautiful Lady. From the children's viewpoint, the marvelous Vision reveals more than greets the eye.

Experts in the field of child psychology keep reminding us that background and environment go a long way to explain the character and behavior of the growing boy or girl. Perhaps the two little shepherds favored with the vision of Our Lady, September 19, 1846, reveal much of their personality under observation made in the light of modern psychology. At any rate, they disclose an attitude and a mode of reacting that help us realize the strange role they shared as co-witnesses of the marvelous event.

It is interesting to recall the early environment and other antecedents which stamped the character of these two children and set in motion the impelling forces of their lives. We note that both Maximin and Melanie, previous to the day of the Apparition, were normal shepherds marked with the distinctive traits and habits of average Alpine folk. They were two peasant youngsters born of needy parents.

Their family rearing had been quite neglected. They had enjoyed hardly any instruction and had been pretty much left to shift for themselves along the lines of rather limited interests. On the eve of the great event, as on any other day, they led their cattle to pasture and were taken up with the routine details of their lowly occupation. They spent most of the time wandering over the steep slopes of Mount Planeau, diverting themselves at shepherds' games and at meal time conversing idly with other shepherds on matters of trifling importance. Never in the least did they suspect the tremendous happening in store for them.

Bereft of most of the charms and advantages of her age, the girl Melanie at the time of the Apparition presented none too alluring a picture. Hers was a dreary and monotonous existence. As already mentioned, her education had been amazingly overlooked. From earliest childhood she had been sent out to beg bread for herself and the family. She learned, in the school of hard reality, how to accept the minimum of prosperity and forego the ease and well-being that make a home and contribute to the human development of a child.

Luxuries were unknown in the Calvat hearth. The girl never tasted the keen joy found in the bosom of a large family brought up in security. Misery and poverty were her first life-companions. These left on her the imprint which she bore to the last. Unsettled at home, she was to spend most of her days shifting from country to country in a career of checkered adventure. This trait indicates that she lacked any kind of preparation to play an important role in whatever situation or state of life she might choose.

As soon as the child Melanie reached the age of usefulness, she was hired as shepherdess on various farms in neighboring villages. This manner of life never allowed her to go to school. Now and then she did appear in church and at Catechism class. So slow was she at learning that at the age of fourteen she could not even recite the *Our Father* or the *Hail Mary*.

Deprived of elementary instruction, she could neither read nor write. A casual listener, she had only a fragmentary understanding of French spoken in ordinary conversation. These sad deficiencies in her formation confirm the notion that the girl appeared radically inept to play a leading role in the great event with which she was to be connected. Her early life had no influence in developing tendencies of self-reliance to face normal life successfully.

As for the boy Maximin, the picture varies little. Unlike Melanie, he had never left the parental roof for any noticeable period, yet this was scarcely an advantage to him. He had lost his mother at a tender age, and his father had remarried. The lad had much to endure on the part of his stepmother, who spared him no occasion of sensing her dislike and coldness. To escape unsympathetic surroundings, the boy, urged by inborn giddiness, was more often out on the road than at home. He, too, was destined to an unsettled and precarious course in later life.

From the intellectual and religious viewpoint, he was a bit more fortunate than Melanie. His stepmother sent him to school and Catechism class, but she failed to keep track of his attendance. The lad took advantage of this lack of supervision. His appearance at class was phenomenally rare and irregular. His progress at study was insignificant. No better prepared was he than Melanie to become the propagator and the collaborator in a mission as important as that entrusted to him on September 19, 1846.

Worth noting is the extreme diversity of character that manifested itself in the two children. The girl Melanie craved solitude and seclusion. Unable to make the effort to appear sociable, she played the dumb, morose and disagreeable poor-mixer. And Maximin hated nothing more than being left alone. Solitude weighed upon him. He needed constant companionship and games. This difference of temperament is another guarantee of their respective sincerity in the role they were to play as witnesses of the Apparition.

Normal Reaction

Faithful to the rendezvous they had arranged the day previous, Maximin and Melanie met soon after breakfast that bright Saturday morning at the crossroad of Ablandins. Breathing the cool mountain air, they climbed the steep path and took their respective flocks to their masters' fields. Nothing extraordinary happened during the forenoon.

When the Angelus struck at twelve noon in the village church steeple, they immediately led their cattle to drink at the Beasts' Spring in a ravine enclosure and then drove them up to recline on the gentle slope of Mount Gargas. Relieved of present cares, they came down to the Men's Spring to take their noon-hour collation. Their frugal meal over, they chatted at ease with a few other shepherds who had come to drink at the spring. When these had gone, they gathered the remnants of their scanty lunch and stored them away, Melanie in her knapsack and Maximin in the folds of his blouse. These they laid down on a stone bench a few steps below in the bed of a dried-up spring.

There was nothing unusual in this routine procedure. The unaccustomed thing that happened was the children's sudden surrender to a deep sleep, which lasted, as they recalled, between one hour and an hour and a half. Here we note the first change that broke the trend of their day. Neither the heat of the afternoon nor the physical exertion of the morning, and still less the light lunch they had nibbled at, could have induced this profound and unbroken slumber.

It was not customary among shepherds on watch to indulge in the siesta hour. The sleep which overtook them was not as natural as we might at first surmise. It may have been sent in the design of Providence to predispose the two witnesses and set them in a restful and calm state of mind, the better to absorb the extraordinary occurrence which was to unfold before them.

The children themselves were at a loss to account for their prolonged nap. A visiting clergyman once questioned Melanie on the matter: "What happened after you had taken your lunch?" Melanie replied: "We fell asleep." "Ah! you said to each other, "'We've got to rest?'"" "No, sir, we fell asleep just like that."

Maximin was likewise questioned: "Was it customary for you to go to sleep after lunch?" "Oh, no, sir, never!" "How come that you both slept that day?" "That, I don't know." What are we to draw from these remarks? We conclude that this strange sleep, so contrary to the children's habit, cannot be explained by the ordinary disposition of their normal psychology.

Observe how prompt they were to adapt themselves to the realities of the conscious state. As soon as they awoke, their conscience tormented them at the memory of the cattle they had left untended. It is not at all astonishing that they thus reacted. Taking in the situation at a glance, they sensed peculiar anguish at the prospect of the reception that awaited them that night at their masters' homes.

In psychological jargon, the thought was "eminently objective" and connected to a practical order of things. It could well evoke in their minds an impressive episode of their past lives, some recent ordeal undergone at sundown, the rod or a streamlined supper, a bit tragic, perhaps, but effective nonetheless.

That this sort of premonition urged them on is shown in the answer they gave Abbé Lagier when he questioned them so closely on every detail of the eventful day. Said Melanie: "I awoke Maximin. When he got up I said to him, 'Come, quick, Maximin, we must go and look for our cows – I don't know where they can be.'"

Maximin echoes her report: "Melanie called me and told me to come right away because we had lost our cattle. Not knowing where they might be, we went to look for them." We gather from this that the two shepherds were quite conscious of their duty and had at heart to perform it faithfully. It is a testimony in their favor, and a guarantee that they spoke sincerely.

Since the boy Maximin had only been "loaned" to Pierre Selme for an occasional trial as shepherd, there is no doubt that the lad wished to return to his father with a favorable report for the week's work. As a rule his master required that the boy return to his side each day after taking the cattle to drink. True, that day he had relied on Melanie to keep watch over Maximin. Nevertheless, the boy was worried about his failure to tend his cattle and return home early.

After spying their cattle resting peacefully on the opposite slope of Mount Gargas, the two shepherds felt more at ease. They came down the hillock in order to pick up their provisions by the stone bench in the ravine, take their cows out to pasture, and then return home. Melanie said to Maximin: "Let's quickly get our knapsacks and take our cows to pasture."

Again the words show their awareness of things and a sober appreciation of their duty. Now, all of a sudden, Melanie halts in her tracks as if nailed to the spot. What had happened? A globe of light, appearing as though "the sun had fallen there," shone over the stone bench near which lay their knapsacks.

Naturally the girl was stunned. "Maximin!" she cried in utter astonishment, "come and see a bright light!" and Maximin, who had dallied on his way down, rushed immediately to her side to view the unusual sight. At first they saw but a dense ball of light that whirled on its axis with dizzying speed, so sparkling that it gave the impression of a wheel in swift rotation.

So seized were the children at this extraordinary phenomenon that they did not even dream of flight, and Melanie dropped her shepherd stick to the ground. Have they lost consciousness or lapsed into a mesmeric trance? Not in the least. Their sensibility is momentarily overwhelmed and paralyzed, for it is a psychological law that violent sensations hamper the functioning of the higher faculties. If anything, however, their attention was sharpened and they gained a keener awareness of reality. There was no deep change or reorientation of their behavior, no break in their line of thought.

Their senses were simply shocked into quick reaction under the stimulation of a strange appearance. They were moved with a natural curiosity to face danger if necessary to comprehend the unexpected light.

It is true that Melanie dropped her shepherd stick, a movement which Maximin perceived immediately. She was subject to fright, but her fear was not as great as might at first appear. The girl herself confirmed this when she said to Abbé Lagier: "We had stopped when we perceived the light and we were a bit afraid." Dropping her stick was merely the result of nervous reaction. She proved that her temperament differed from that of Maximin. Interiorly, he was perhaps more agitated than Melanie. His remonstrance was "Keep your stick! I'll keep mine and I shall give it a good whack if it does us anything." This does not necessarily convince us of his bravery.

Upon first perceiving the strong light in the ravine of the Apparition, the girl Melanie recalled a rebuke she frequently had heard from the lips of old Mother Caron. The unusual globe of light brought back to her memory the threat that "some day, if she refused to say her prayers and went on laughing at those who prayed she surely would see the devil."

There is a psychological reason for this sudden reminiscence. A child of fourteen years knows nothing of the occult powers of nature. Ignorant mountain folk, isolated from the outside world, are generally inclined to superstitious belief in the signs read in shooting stars, strange dreams and stories of diabolical exploits. Melanie had no doubt heard such stories, some of them pleasant and amusing, others fantastic and terrifying.

It is no wonder, then, that the repeated threats of her old mistress awoke in her a serious apprehension that the light might hold a spirit about to materialize. By the sheer power of association of ideas, this picture stood on the threshold of her consciousness. Psychology explains it thus: under the provocation of certain circumstances kindred conditions of mind have a tendency to revive and find exterior expression.

Quite similar, in a way, was the reaction registered by the boy Maximin. His first thought upon discerning a woman in the globe of light was to identify her with some woman or other from the neighboring hamlet of Valjouffrey. The strange light lay over the stone bench near which the children had left their provision kits. The lad instinctively believed that a woman had ventured on the premises and was somehow interested in the shepherds' knapsacks – intent, perhaps, upon taking away their meager rations. The report jotted down by Abbé Lagier lends credence of a sort to Maximin's early suspicion.

"Did you think it was some lady or some woman or other?"

"Yes, I thought it was some lady and that the sun made the pretty things she wore shine brightly."

"Did you think that she might have come from some place near by?"

"Yes."

"Where from?"

"From Valjouffrey."

It might seem that the Abbé's question suggested a reply in the sense desired; yet it was not Maximin's practice to answer questions just to please the questioner. His surmise concerning the identity of the lady was but transitory, however, since when asked again by the inquisitive Abbé whether he persevered in this belief, the boy replied that while listening to the Beautiful Lady he was too much absorbed to do anything else but drink in her words.

"Now tell me – when she spoke to you that way (alluding to the heavy arm of her Son) you still thought she was a lady from Valjouffrey?"

"We said nothing. I thought of nothing. There we stood – just listening."

On some other occasion another gentleman questioned Maximin in a like vein. He learned that the boy held more than one notion as to who the strange personage might be.

"Did you know that it was the Blessed Virgin who was speaking to you?"

"No, sir."

"Who then did you think it might be?"

"I thought it was some woman who had been beaten by her son and had fled into the mountain."

In February, 1847, Melanie was also questioned by Abbé Lagier and in the main her reply scarcely varied from that of Maximin. She did not identify the Lady in any clearer fashion than might be expected of her.

"Didn't you think it was perhaps some woman from Valjouffrey?"

"I didn't know what to think. We just listened to her."

It appears that the two children retained normal control of their imaginative powers and were not affected by the light or the Lady in any way that might have deprived them of ordinary conscious reaction.

REALM OF SIGHT

The same normalcy applies in regard to the children's ability to view the person within the mysterious globe of light. Their eyesight remained reliably clear throughout the Apparition. Despite the dazzling brightness that filled their field of vision, they noted with precision the varied phases of the wonder unfolding before them. And when the light parted they perceived, as it were, the vague form of two hands closely joined. At first, these hands were none too neatly delineated, and brilliant pearls were gleaming near them.

Only by degrees did the children discern the successive traits and features of the Beautiful Lady. Soon the sketchy pair of hands grew densely white and assumed a more definite outline, so that Melanie could say, "We gathered that they were really hands." A crown of roses also appeared around these hands. These roses were part of the diadem on the Lady's brow, which rested in her open palms. Then as the arms and elbows came into view, her long sleeves and part of her dress bearing sparkling pearls became more distinct.

Suddenly the light rose to a person's height, the arms of the Lady folded one over the other, and the children saw her stand upright.

Melanie described each stage of the strange phenomenon. Her perception, a bit confused at first, gained in strength and clarity until she fully grasped the vision of the Lady present before them.

From Maximin's viewpoint, the process seems to have unfurled in reverse order. At least that was his manner of reporting it. "All of a sudden," he said, "we saw a Lady; then the globe of light lowered and expanded." Doubtless he indicates that the light around her person thinned out so as to leave her more easily visible within the dense, luminous globe.

There is no real contradiction in the children's diverse modes of describing the vision. We observe that as a rule Maximin preferred to draw a brief portrayal rather than indulge in the minute scrutiny of details. The lad's visual perception was quite as rich as Melanie's, but his word picture of what he saw proceeded by way of abridgment. While Melanie enlarged upon the accidentals of the scene, Maximin fixed his attention on the broad essentials. The difference lies in the mode of retrospection peculiar to each witness.

Maximin was also more affirmative than Melanie. At times the girl witness expressed herself with a tone of reserve and hesitancy. By contrast, the lad always spoke out categorically. Compare these two declarations regarding the position and attitude of the Beautiful Lady when she was first observed. Maximin says: "The Lady was seated on a stone bench on which we had sat. Her elbows were resting on her knees. Her face was hidden in her hands." Note how less emphatic is Melanie's report: "We saw her arms and elbows, but we did not distinguish the rest of her person very clearly. It seemed as though she was seated."

The children were particularly observant about the nature and quality of the luminous globe which encircled them and the Lady during the Apparition. This encompassing light surpassed in splendor that of the sun on that cloudless afternoon in September. The two shepherds were aware of the sunlight, but only by way of contrast. It paled and waned in comparison with the spotless radiance of the Vision. The oval hearth of celestial light was less intense than the brightness which emanated from the person of the Beautiful Lady.

The witnesses remarked that her very apparel and adornment were woven, so to speak, out of the rays that seemed to issue from her body – the glorified body of Heaven's Queen. Among the shining objects which she wore, the Christ on the cross was brightest of all. Writes Father Bossan on this matter: "This cross with the figure of Christ and the hammer and pliers shone like bright gold, but the cross was brighter than the hammer and tongs, and the figure of Christ was still more luminous than the cross."

Unlike the sunlight, the radiance of the globe was heatless and cast no shadow. The children were within touching distance of her person, yet felt no discomfort from the powerful light beaming upon them. Melanie pointed out that neither the Lady nor they themselves cast any shadow. "The Lady cast no shadow about her; as for us, when we were apart from her, we did cast our own shadow, but there was no shadow when we were near her."

Besides their ability to visualize the details of the appearance before them, we note their equal skill in determining the general color pattern of the Vision they attempted to portray. They observed the pale coloring of the sunlight in contrast to the fiery glow of the strange ball of light in the ravine. They also described the identical pattern of white and gold, which formed the color scheme of the Vision, with variations in multicolored rose wreaths.

Their casual inventory is summed up as follows: white low shoes, golden buckles, white dress and kerchief, golden apron, golden chains and cross, white headdress, white pearls, and rose garlands of every hue. This kind of color fixation, proved by parallel testimonies, shows that the two witnesses possessed keen and watchful eyesight. Their vision was not seriously hampered by the sparkling light in which they themselves stood.

In regard to Maximin, however, an amazing exception must be noted. Unlike Melanie, try as he might, he was unable to scan the

Beautiful Lady's visage. He admitted that he could not make out exactly how she looked. A veil of shimmering light, hovering from her lips to her brow, seemed to interfere with his vision. Melanie alone had the happiness of contemplating at ease the Virgin's ravishing features. This strange fact is quite beyond psychological interpretation. Why, may we ask, was the lad prevented from viewing the face of the Weeping Mother? We must invoke a mysterious design of the Beautiful Lady, which fairly escapes the critic's exacting mind.

During the Apparition the children were exceptionally alert in reckoning positions, distances, direction and general orientation. They were able to retrace, step by step, the movements of the Beautiful Lady. They averred that they stood so near to her that no other person could have come in between them and her.

When the Lady had finished her discourse, she crossed the brook and slowly ascended the knoll facing her. "We crossed the brook after her and followed her closely," reported Melanie. They adapted their movements and their progress with her own. They were drawn after her by an irresistible attraction. When the Lady made a slight detour to climb the winding path leading to the summit of the knoll, Melanie went directly ahead and preceded her in such wise as to stand facing her when she reached the top. Maximin, at that moment, was still a few yards down on the slope of the mound.

The children also closely observed her manner of walking. "She walked above the grass, without pressing it down." Maximin, in the circumstance, experienced a momentary dread; noting that the Lady was setting out to walk up the slope, he was afraid she might ruin the roses around her footwear. To his great relief, the Lady's feet scarcely grazed the light mountain grass and the flowers in her path.

This exquisite regard on the part of the shepherd lad manifests his solicitous interest in the Beautiful Lady. He so cherished her beauty that he feared lest anything unexpected should mar her charms.

In his place we would have entertained no other sentiment.

At the moment of the Lady's disappearance, the reaction on the children's part was one of disappointment. She had risen from the ground at the level of their heads, and there remained suspended for a brief instant. Then suddenly her head vanished in the heavens, then her arms and the rest of her body. Nothing was left but the roses at her feet. Leaping toward these, the boy flung out his hand to grasp a rose and to his dismay discovered that it melted in his hand "like butter in a pan."

There was still a great light at the spot where she had disappeared, but this, too, vanished before their eyes, with a last flickering glow. The two shepherds stood still, entranced, but after realizing all was over, they fell to discussing the Vision in their own naïve and innocent fashion. They felt deep contentment and happiness, but little understood the full import of what they had seen and heard.

REALM OF SOUND

Clear and immediate perception favored the two witnesses in regard to the sound of the Beautiful Lady's voice. "Come near, my children," she said to them as they stood transfixed on the knoll, "be not afraid, I am here to tell you great news." These words spoken with alluring gentleness swiftly allayed their apprehension. Readily did the two shepherds rush down to meet her as she took a few steps along the bed of the dried-up spring. The mere sound of her voice had won and captivated them.

An inquisitive pilgrim, a Mr. Gabier, once queried Maximin about the voice of the strange Lady. "Regarding the sound of her voice, it seems that you did not hear it quite distinctly. Now, no mistake about it, you really heard her voice?"

"Why, certainly, we did hear her voice, very clearly; but it is impossible to give an exact idea of so harmonious a sound."

In the sound of Mary's voice the children discerned a tonal quality which they acknowledged themselves powerless to describe. In their effort to do so they exhausted all the comparisons at their command. "The sound of her voice resembled music... her voice was sweet as music... we seemed to eat up her words instantly... she wept, yet her voice was extremely pleasant." The voice sounded incomparably rich and sonorous, soft and modulated in harmony with the content of her words.

Her message was lyrical with celestial melody. Said Melanie: "Her words struck my ears in a manner that I cannot define; each sound held a soft, flowing cadence, and her words settled immediately in my memory." With exquisite harmony, known only to heaven, Mary etched her message deep into the minds of her ravished listeners.

The voice of the Beautiful Lady was in no way comparable to that of other women. Maximin once explained this to the Mother Superior of the Convent at Corps, where he had been admitted for particular instruction. Said the boy: "Her voice was sweet – sweeter than that of Sister V." Sister V was perhaps the singing teacher at the Convent. It is obvious that the lad did not make this comparison at the time of the Apparition. He spoke thus to show how futile was any attempt to describe the Lady's voice adequately. Even those who heard the voice of the Sister alluded to could form but the vaguest notion of the inimitable voice which charmed the two Alpine shepherds on September 19, 1846.

So fair and entrancing was Our Lady's voice, so resonant with sad yet soothing music, that all the melody in the world, all church instruments, choirs and symphonies could but displease for a long time thereafter the musical sense of the two witnesses.

After several years of traveling and experience, Maximin, haunted with the nostalgia of Mary's voice, sighed longingly to himself, "Never will I hear anything so beautiful!" He yearned to hearken once again to the penetrating music of the sweet, maternal voice that had lulled and subdued him during that brief heavenly interval.

From our cursory survey in the realm of light and sound, we gather that the two lowly witnesses of Mary's Apparition, while taken up entirely with the contemplation of the Beautiful Lady, failed not to observe with normal ability the external display of the Vision they were privileged to behold. They were fully aware of the environment and setting of the dramatic occasion.

Nothing escaped their visual and auditory perception. They manifested extreme suppleness in the range and quality of their sense reactions. True to their instinctive and native characters, they proved themselves fit and apt instruments to fulfill the design of the Merciful Mother of La Salette.

REALM OF EMOTION

It is interesting to note the emotional reactions on the part of the two witnesses of La Salette during their privileged experience. As soon as they heard the Beautiful Lady's invitation, "Come near, my children, do not be afraid," they dashed down the slope of the ravine to take their stand in front of her. Children are spontaneously drawn toward anything that charms and glitters. In their avid curiosity they do not discuss or question this natural tendency. If an object but please them, they fix their whole attention upon it.

Thus the boy Maximin was so captivated by the Lady in the globe of light that he was quite unaware of his quaint and negligent appearance. Certainly he doffed his wide-brimmed hat in the presence of the strange personage, but he stood there blissfully oblivious that he had not got back into his shepherd blouse. This detail is gently touched over by artists who take care to represent the lad fully groomed for the occasion...

Fascinated by the shining vision, the two children stood together, facing the extraordinary visitor. She was so close to them that they could have touched her. In their transport of admiration, they did not fail to reckon the slight distance which separated them from her. They observed that another person could not have stepped in between them. They were all eyes and ears as we might expect from children of sound and normal emotional background.

Their first attitude had been one of mingled fear and caution. This uncertainty was but the initial phase of voluntary choice. Upon hearing the Lady's sweet words of welcome, they knew as if by instinct that a good thing was at hand. They sensed the benevolent intention of the afflicted Mother. They became subdued and attentive. They did not even wish to offer the least resistance. From a feeling of vague hesitancy and a first attempt at self-defense, they passed to complete security and total surrender.

In cases of diabolical manifestations it has been observed that the feeling first conveyed is rather one of elation and unwarranted joy, which all too soon ends in fright and anxiety of mind. It was not so with the children, Melanie and Maximin. On the contrary, after a passing dread of the unknown, there followed a pleasant and inexpressible sentiment of peace – in their own words, "a great content and happiness," which they were never again to experience as long as they lived. The vision became the central interest of their conscious state. All other ideas and feelings remained on the fringe of their emotional activity.

The children's attention did not increase the intensity of the vision which ravished them. The appearance was so radiant and sparkling that they could not add to its content. They could merely glimpse it, yet not without a certain effort on their part. Melanie reported to Abbé Lagier: "We could hardly see her, she dazzled us so." Maximin said: "When I looked at her she nearly blinded my eyes so that I could hardly look at her closely." This was due to the excessive brightness of the light, which momentarily affected their vision.

With some people, intense concentration leads to the defective exercise of their faculty of observation, if not to the total cessation of effort. The children, however, were well aware of their actual mood and condition. In all simplicity they said: "We just stood there and listened," indicating the perfect normalcy of their emotional make-up.

It cannot be said that they were the victims of hallucination or of a mountain-caused mirage. They were too keenly strung and wide-awake to be thus deceived. They exerted enough initiative to warrant the reality of what they saw and heard. Neither were they bewitched or mesmerized. In fact, their ability to move freely is seen in their changing posture and their varied gestures. In no way were their movements dictated by exterior coercion or suggestion.

When the Lady spoke a secret to Melanie, moving her lips but making no audible sound for Maximin, the lad amused himself during the prolonged interval by twirling his hat on the end of his shepherd staff or knocking pebbles about with his stick, sending them rolling near the feet of the Beautiful Lady. When she again addressed herself to both children simultaneously, he resumed his attitude of earnest attention.

To say that the children lacked liberty of action is contradicted by the fact that they enjoyed sufficient freedom to raise their hands and rub their eyes. By wiping off a sort of mistiness which dimmed their sight, they could thus momentarily obtain a clearer view of the Lady wrapped in light.

Said Melanie: "We kept rubbing our eyes and then looked on more closely." Maximin had serious trouble in trying to view the features of the Lady. In fact, a kind of shimmering glare concealed her face, from her lips to her brow. More fortunate than her companion, Melanie was able to glimpse them clearly enough. "Her face was sad," she said. "I did see it distinctly two or three times." Thus it is shown that the children did exert free, physical and voluntary efforts to center their gaze upon the Vision. They were not in any way numbed or paralyzed into inactivity nor unduly influenced by some external force.

We need not minimize the role played by the faculty of memory in the children's transmission of Mary's message. It is true that the two witnesses were singularly lacking in elementary education, yet they were by no means a pair of witless waifs. Brought up in the hard school of necessity, they held fast to solid, earthly common sense. We cannot overlook this basic and sane endowment of nature. This sound mental quality made them apt instruments to accomplish the mission which Our Lady confided to them.

It follows that the two shepherds were not mere machines, able only to register what they heard, like a recording. Passive they were in their receptive attitude, yet their minds contributed the necessary share of activity to grasp and transmit the thoughts and images conveyed to them. We should not exaggerate the part of miraculous intervention in this regard. Every instance in which they manifest individual and intelligent initiative confirms their testimony. Otherwise we might be tempted to believe that they had been prompted and coached to stage a fictitious role in some monstrous hoax.

People who heard the children recite the story of the Apparition often remarked that they showed a rare facility in repeating Our Lady's discourse. They seemed to rattle off her words with the ease of schoolchildren telling a tale learned by rote. This was all the more striking when we consider that the little shepherds had but a vague and limited knowledge of French.

However, the contrary would have been just as startling. It is plain that frequent repetition certainly gave them greater versatility in their manner of speech. This goes to prove that their natural gifts were not stunted, and that they freely and normally performed their task as intelligent broadcasters, "making it known to all her people."

Closing her conversation with the shepherds of La Salette, the

Beautiful Lady related a remarkable episode in the life of the boy, Maximin. In view of the supernatural element involved, the incident of the Farm of Coin presents an interesting angle in the psychology of the shepherd-witnesses.

The Blessed Virgin asked them if they had ever seen spoiled wheat. Not knowing which of them she was addressing, the little girl replied softly, in a muffled tone of voice, "No, Madam, we have never seen any." Melanie had in fact never seen spoiled wheat. Maximin had seen some once out in the fields with his father, but he had completely forgotten the incident. The Blessed Virgin recalled it to his mind.

The episode of the Farm of Coin opens, as it were, a new vista into the realm of the children's psychology. It is a bit startling to note Maximin's reply to Our Lady's question, "Have you never seen spoiled wheat, my children?" "No, Madam, we have never seen any."

The sight of spoiled wheat should have left a vivid impression on the child. The Lady's words should have evoked a tragic scene in the lad's memory. Yet his temporary forgetfulness runs true to pattern and shows how very much "himself" he remained throughout the Lady's appearance and discourse.

Certain interests in life hold greater appeal than others and are apt to revive in the memory by virtue of kindred association. We know that Mr. Giraud, Maximin's father, was a wheelwright by trade. The son was apparently destined to follow in his footsteps and was initiated in the first contacts of that occupation.

The lad was a town boy and, unlike a farmer's boy, took little interest in reckoning the yield of the fields, the effects of drought or rain, and seasons of dearth or plenty. His earliest environment was his father's carpentry shop, where he breathed the atmosphere of his parent's business. The mere mention of spoiled wheat awakes few souvenirs in his mind. Even repetition could hardly stamp the image into his ungrateful faculty. Time could easily erase the picture from the rough tablet of his imagination.

When the incident of the Farm of Coin took place, young Maximin gave it no more than passing heed. His flighty character and irresponsible nature called for no further consideration of the matter. It was necessary for his father to stress the meaning of the tragic circumstance.

Halting about halfway on the road home, he gave the lad a piece of bread, saying, "Eat some bread this year at least, my child; if the wheat continues to spoil like this, I do not know who will eat any next year." This reference to a vital need served to anchor the remark somewhere in the boy's treacherous memory. Yet only serious reflection could draw it to the surface of consciousness. At the moment of the Apparition, the child was so absorbed in viewing the Beautiful Lady and so subdued by her words that he made no effort to give a pondered answer to her question.

Pausing briefly to allow time for self-examination, the Beautiful Lady proceeded to help the boy remember the forgotten incident. It was a matter of digging out a memory from the grave of oblivion. Very gently, by means of a series of precise, piecemeal and concrete details, she made him relive the dramatic scene and drew from him this naïve confession, "Oh, yes, Madam, that is very true; just now I did not remember." It is doubtful, at best, whether the lost souvenir would ever have recurred to him without the delicate prodding of Our Lady's reminiscent words, buried deep in a dim corner of his subconscious mind.

Slowly reviewing the events of that distant afternoon near the Farm of Coin and on the road to Corps, she directed his mind toward the proper channels of recollection. In this disclosure of a forgotten incident, one thing stands out in bold relief; the lad reacted in natural conformity with his individual character, which stamped him as a plain and unspoiled child of the hills. His spontaneous admission was along the line of development we first noted in his psychological pattern – a strong sense of adaptation to reality.

Next we note something which overflows the limits of psychological laws. What astonishes the expert here is the strange manner in which the reviviscence of a buried memory was effected. There would be nothing unusual to remark if the incident of the Farm of Coin had been brought back to the boy's mind either by his father or by the other person involved, the owner of the field. The fact, too, that the Beautiful Lady was intimately familiar with the dual scene enacted on that distant day, at the farm of Coin and midway on the road to Corps, surpasses all human explanation.

The known witnesses of the episode could alone have divulged it. So far as can be ascertained, only the father and the lad knew of both incidents. Surely it is not Maximin who informed the Lady of it, since it is she who reminded him of it. Neither was it the father, since when told of the Lady's knowledge of the event he was so stunned by the inexplicable allusion that, then and there, he gave full credence to the lad's report of the Apparition, notwithstanding his previous violent hostility.

Expert psychologists concede their inability to furnish a satisfying solution to the problem. The revelation was a phenomenon which derived from a power above the realm of nature.

REALM OF INTELLECT

Our Lady's first words to the children were spoken in French. If the two shepherds had absolutely no previous acquaintance with the language and understood nothing but their local dialect, how could they so readily respond to her invitation? The softness and kindliness of her voice could not fully explain their change of attitude to one of trust and eagerness. Children understand a pleasant call, even from a stranger, but when frightened by unknown persons speaking an unfamiliar tongue their doubts are not so easily dispelled.

It must be that Our Lady's words carried a definite meaning to their minds. What little French they knew sufficed at the moment for their understanding. Her gentle words, "Come near, do not be afraid," calmed their troubled hearts. Instantly they felt the warmth and confidence of a mother toward them.

Hence, as Melanie says, "As soon as she told us to come near we ran down promptly; we crossed the brook in front of her and we were no longer afraid, and we went down to meet her." Both had grasped the significance of her spoken words and felt that more was to be told, which they were able dimly to comprehend. "I am here to tell you great news," the Lady had said.

People were also surprised to note certain changes in the wording of the children's recital. Thus Melanie persistently used the expression, "the hand of my Son," and Maximin, "the arm of my Son." For example: "I shall be forced to let fall the hand of my Son" and "the arm of my Son is so strong and so heavy that I can no longer withhold it." They never departed from this unusual procedure. There is nothing really astounding in such a detail, yet some persons did not like these alterations in the rendition of Our Lady's discourse.

It is quite impossible, of course, to determine which term was uttered by Our Lady when speaking her message. It is sufficient to hold that each witness grasped the real sense of her words, regardless. The witnesses gathered the notion of chastisement, and each expressed it in terms best suited to his or her temperament and psychology. The precise idea of "correction" in a girl's mind is closely allied to that of a hand raised to strike the culprit; in a boy's experience it evokes the more formidable picture of a strong arm ready to apply the stick.

"Did you understand what she meant when she said the 'hand of my Son'?" asked Abbé Lagier in his judicious interview with Melanie. The girl replied: "I did not understand exactly what she meant" – that is to say, she did not know whose son was in the Lady's mind – but she added, "I did grasp a little of everything."

Maximin gave a clue to their mystification: "I thought it was some mother who had been beaten by her son and had been forced to flee into the mountain wilderness, and I figured she had received many a heavy blow." There is no questioning the fact that the two little shepherds, so enraptured by the voice of the Beautiful Lady, did not fail to seize the intelligible content of her words.

If the children were able to follow the general meaning of Our Lady's discourse spoken in French, they certainly grasped still more easily and readily that portion of her message which she delivered in the plain dialect of the region. They felt no need to call for an explanation of the familiar patois.

When the Beautiful Lady asked them, "Do you pray well, my children?" they promptly replied, "Not very well, Madam." Evidently they had at least a vague notion of prayer and admitted their want of assiduity in the practice of it. Then, too, when mention was made of the ruined wheat, they momentarily failed to recall previous acquaintance with the phenomenon, but they understood that she was referring to things within the range of their experience.

Regarding Our Lady's final injunction, twice repeated in French, here again we note their manner of seizing the obvious sense of the commission entrusted to them. "Well, my children, you will make this known to all my people" were the parting words of the heavenly visitor. The children could not but sense that they were invested with a special mission toward all people.

That very night, at their respective masters' homes, they broke the great news of the event and rehearsed the striking message in the presence of the members of their humble household. From that day on they never wearied of telling their story to all comers, and they faithfully discharged their task in the same matter-of-fact manner indicated by the direct words of the Beautiful Lady.

In her interesting volume, *"Echo of the Holy Mountain"*, Miss Marie Des Brulais (1809-1896) brings out the alertness of the children's minds in this respect. "What did you understand," asked the author, "when the Blessed Virgin told you to make it known to all her people?" Melanie answered, "I understood that I must tell it to all." "But how do you take the word 'people'? Do you think that Our Lady meant the inhabitants of this country only?" Melanie: "I wouldn't know – but I understood that she meant everybody."

That the witnesses showed keen mental alertness in grasping the meaning of Our Lady's discourse is brought out in her reference to ruined crops. "If the harvest is spoilt, it is all on your account. I gave you warning last year in the potatoes, but you did not heed it. On the contrary, when you found the potatoes spoilt, you swore, you took the name of my Son in vain. They will continue to decay, so that by Christmas there will be none left." These words, spoken in French, were a rebuke to the farmers of the region, yet the children seized their general content, except for a single word which mystified the girl, Melanie, the French word for potato, *pomme-de-terre,* which roughly rendered means *"ground-apple."*

In the dialect of Corps the familiar expression is *truffas*. We can well imagine Melanie's wonder at the mention of apples found in the ground. In her bewilderment she bestirred herself to seek light on the matter. She was about to turn toward Maximin and ask him the meaning of *pomme-de-terre*. Noticing her intention, the Beautiful Lady spared her the trouble by repeating that part of her discourse in the patois of Corps.

It is evident that up to that point Melanie had understood the general gist of the Lady's words, otherwise her attempt to solve the puzzle of *pomme-de-terre* could have no real motive. Her desire to miss nothing of what she heard prompted her to risk interrupting the Lady's soft-flowing discourse.

All this is quite in conformity with the mental pattern of this peasant girl. We may ask why she did not inquire of the Lady herself what the strange word was intended to convey. No doubt it was respect for the Beautiful Lady which forbade her to do so. All the girl meant to do was to whisper her request on the side, without interfering or letting the Lady observe her demeanor.

At no time during the conversation did the children take the initiative by addressing the Lady. She provoked replies to a few queries, but her attentive listeners were quite content to lend their ears to her enthralling discourse. Their attitude was that of shy children in the presence of strangers. Timid youngsters avoid marks of forwardness, as do even grownups, upon meeting great personages.

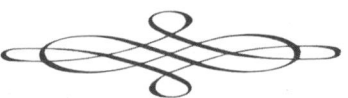

When the Beautiful Lady had vanished into the azure light of the Alpine sky, the children sought in vain for a last lingering glimpse of the marvelous vision. Nothing was left to them but the sun's lengthening rays across the rocky mountain slopes, the grandiose frame of rugged hills, the sharp serrated rim of the surrounding peaks fringing the horizon with silver and purple edge, the soft languor and mystery of the quiet solitude; the two young shepherds were brought back to earth with abrupt suddenness to face the plain routine of their daily chores. Yet in their hearts dwelt a deep and unutterable bliss.

"As soon as the Beautiful Lady disappeared," said Melanie, "we went down to pick up our knapsacks and return to our cattle." This direct reporting to duty is evidence that the children were fully aware of the actual situation they were in. There was no break or cleavage in the trend of their psychological activity, but rather a continuous flow of reaction to reality. And so, while returning to their cattle, they naturally exchanged impressions.

Melanie said, "Wasn't she all so lovely? She must be a great saint – she rose up into the air!" Maximin shrugged his shoulders. "I wouldn't know!" Not knowing what to make of it, he had only one regret, that of no longer being able to see the Beautiful Lady. On their way back to the village, Maximin and Melanie spoke of the vision to none of the shepherds they passed on the road. They held fast to their solitary dream of beauty and clutched at the memory of it with simple and unshakable faith.

We discover a charming trait of child psychology in their first talk about the Lady's confidential disclosures to each of them during her discourse. Maximin, with usual playfulness, taunts Melanie about it. "My, she ceased talking for quite awhile! I could see her lips moving though. What was she saying when she said nothing?" Melanie replied, "She did tell me something but I won't tell it to you, she forbade me to."

A bit piqued, Maximin answered in similar vein, "Oh, how glad I am, Melanie! There – she told me something too but I won't tell it to you either." This attitude of mutual reticence bespeaks their real character; Melanie, cagey and morose, and Maximin a bit arrogant but childishly clever in his baffled attempt to make Melanie talk.

That evening, for the first time, each reported the day's great adventure to a different group of listeners. They told the identical story, each from his or her own viewpoint, delivering the Beautiful Lady's discourse with genuine and instinctive alacrity. Thus began their checkered career as messengers of the rapturous Vision on the Mountain. Yet as the years roll on and life shifts the scene of their apostolate, they remain the clear transmitters of the Voice on the Hill calling the people to submission and repentance.

Faithful to the Fair Lady of their love, who had drawn them from their modest herds on the Alpine mountainside, they pursued unfalteringly, true to their native character, the lifelong task of heralding the tearful cry of the new Rachel, "weeping for her children… since they are no more" (Matthew 2:18).